Civil Justice

From the Constitutional Rights Foundation and Scholastic

LIVING LAW

Civil Justice

SCHOLASTIC INC.
New York Toronto London Sydney Auckland Tokyo

Titles in the Living Law Program

Criminal Justice
Civil Justice

ISBN-0-590-00517-0

19 18 17 16 15 14 13 12 11 10 9   4 5 6 7 8/8

Printed in the U. S. A.   23

Staff for the Living Law Program

For the Constitutional Rights Foundation

Author

Susan McKay

Supervisory Editors

Todd Clark
Richard Weintraub

Youth and the Administration of Justice
  Project Staff

Nancy York, Project Director
Todd Clark, Education Advisor
Richard Weintraub, Education Advisor
Sandra Morley, Education Director
Russell Dawkins, Field Coordinator
Brenda Frieberg, Project Coordinator
Ann Senechal, Project Writer

Contents

INTRODUCTION

What is Civil Law?

Look at what's being said in these eight short scenes. Which of them do you think involve the law?

1. "Don't anybody move. This is a stickup!"

2. "The ads said that Sniffo would clear up my stuffy nose instantly. But it didn't do a thing."

3. "I don't care what my parents say. Let's run away and get married."

4. "So it's agreed. Your company won't charge less than $25 a box, and neither will ours."

5. "You told me I'd only have to pay a few dollars a month. But you didn't tell me I'd be paying for four years."

6. "Hey, Jan, you promised I could borrow your bike if I helped you with your homework. What about it?"

7. "Hey, get out of that car — it's mine. . . . Come back!"

8. "Mrs. Smith, your son had some matches and let my little Jimmy play with them. Now Jimmy has burned his hand."

If you decided that all eight scenes involve the law, you are perfectly right. However, they don't all involve the law in the same way.

In three of the scenes, crimes are taking place. No. 1 is a robbery; No. 4, price-fixing; and

No. 7, auto theft. These are considered offenses against society, even though there may be just one victim. When a crime is committed, it is the state that takes action against the accused person. The laws that deal with crimes are known all together as *criminal law*.

The other five scenes involve not criminal law but *civil law*. This is the area of law which deals with the private rights of individuals and with conflicts arising over those rights. A person who thinks that another person (or organization) has violated his or her rights may settle the dispute in court. This is done by filing a civil action (lawsuit*) against the person or organization. Note one basic difference from criminal law — that it is the individual, not the state, that takes legal action.

You may be surprised to discover how much of everyday life is covered by civil law. It deals with the rights of consumers (scenes Nos. 2 and 5) and also with marriage and family life (No. 3). It covers many agreements (No. 6) and also various types of accidents (No. 8). And this is just a beginning.

This book describes some of the

---

*See the Glossary at the back of this book for the meaning of any unusual words.

most important areas of civil law. These are the areas that you are most likely to encounter in your everyday life, either now or in the next few years.

The book is divided into five parts:
• Part 1: Consumer Law. When you pay money to buy something, what rights do you have? This unit shows how the law affects buying and selling, advertising, and borrowing money.
• Part 2: Contract Law. You may think that contracts involve only businessmen and hundreds or thousands of dollars. But that isn't so. This unit shows how a large number of everyday agreements are covered by civil law.
• Part 3: Housing Law. Whether you rent a small apartment or buy your own home, you have certain legal rights and responsibilities.
• Part 4: Accidents and Injuries. There are many different ways in which people can cause harm to others. When are you responsible for an accident? What can you do if someone else harms you?
• Part 5: Family Law. Although family life is a private matter, the law still protects the individuals concerned. This unit examines the laws affecting marriage, divorce, and the relations between parents and children.

What can you gain from studying civil law? There are three main answers to that question.

First, you can acquire a practical knowledge of your legal rights and responsibilities in everyday life. This knowledge can save you money, time, and trouble.

Second, as you go through this book, you will have many opportunities to compare *your* views on legal issues with the views of judges and lawyers. This can give you a clearer understanding of the principles on which the American system of justice is based.

Third, you will discover that the law is not a fixed set of rules but a system that can develop and change. You will see how many laws have changed — and still are changing — to meet the challenges of 20th-century life. And you can start thinking now of ways in which the law might or should change in the future.

This book does more than simply describe the law. It offers you real-life cases, stories, and interviews. It gives you ideas for role-playing situations, suggests experts you can invite to talk with your class, and includes humorous cartoons — as well as serious charts — for testing your knowledge.

In short, this book is designed not just to teach you but also to interest you and challenge you.

PART 1
CONSUMER
LAW

Chapter 1

The New Consumer

The assignment? A cinch!

Agent X chuckled as he unfolded the small piece of paper. On it was a single word. He read it and tossed it aside. It was clear what had to be done.

X stepped outside into the cold misty rain. In minutes, he stood before a small well-lit building. A cold chill passed over him.

X pulled his coat tight around his neck and pushed his way through the door. Inside he was greeted by bright lights and a tall man in a white coat. The man smiled at him. Was it a friendly smile? X couldn't tell.

"Can I help you?" the man asked.

X cleared his throat. "I'll just take a look around."

"Help yourself."

There they were! What he had come for. Dozens of them. All alike — almost.

X picked up one. This could be it. Then he picked up another. So could this . . . or this . . . or this. Was it the large or the small . . . the regular or the economy?

X looked closer. There were messages on some of them. "Top protection!" . . . "Best value!" . . . "The bright choice!" Someone was trying to help him. Or were they trying to confuse him?

X began to grab one after another. Was it mint or spearmint or cinnamon? Was it a whitener or a freshener? With fluoride or not?

"Well?" The man in the white coat sneered.

X froze in his tracks. Then he said, "I need more information."

X knew he had lost — for now. It was time to get out. At the door, he turned around. "I'll be back. You can count on that!"

X strode out into the cold rain. His hands were sweating.

Your Turn

What do you think the story is about? What do you think Agent X was trying to do? What kind of information did Agent X need?

1.
Our consumer economy

As you may have guessed, Agent X was simply trying to choose a tube of toothpaste. What started out as an easy task turned into a nightmare. Of course, very few of us go through such agony every time we buy toothpaste. Still, the choices before Agent X are similar to those faced by millions of Americans every day. Who is Agent X? He is the American consumer. He could be you.

A consumer is someone who buys something or uses a service. Since we all buy things and use services, we are all consumers. There are more than 200 million of us in the U.S. today. And we spend hundreds of billions of dollars to satisfy our needs and wants.

At the same time, businesses spend millions of dollars to find out what the American consumer will buy. As a result, hundreds of new goods and services are offered to us each year.

Consumer law

Clearly, there are advantages to living in a consumer economy such as ours. But there are also problems. Like Agent X, we may find it hard to make the right choices. We may not know enough about the kind of product we want to buy. We may be confused by all the different advertising. We may buy something on "easy credit" and find that it is not easy to pay at all. In all these cases we are cheating ourselves because we don't know enough.

We may also have a problem because someone else is trying to cheat us. The great majority of business people are honest, but some are not. They may not tell the truth about the products they make or sell. They may trick us into making wrong choices or paying more than we can afford.

How can we deal with these problems? Many laws have been made to help us do just that. When we talk about all these laws together, they are known as *consumer law*.

There are two basic aims behind consumer law:

• *To set standards.* For example, foods sold in the U.S. must be of a certain quality. Some foods, like meat, are marked with different grades, so the consumer knows better how to make a choice. In fact, setting standards of *information* is an important part of consumer law.

• *To end dishonest practices.* Today, if you are cheated by a dishonest business person, the chances are you can take legal action against him or her. Of course, the law cannot stop you from cheating yourself. Only you can protect yourself — by becoming an *informed* consumer.

In this unit we will explore some of the areas in which consumer problems often arise. You will learn about special buying skills that can help you become an effective consumer. And you will learn about some of the laws that protect your consumer rights.

Your Turn

You are at your local supermarket. You are looking at a shelf filled with different brands of bath soap, cereal, laundry detergent, or soft drinks. What factors may cause you to buy one brand rather than another? Why do you think a store may offer a variety of brands of the same type of product?

Field Activity

Pick three types of products that can be found on the shelves of your local supermarket. For example, you might pick soft drinks, dog food, and frozen orange juice. Check the size or weight of the different brands and compare prices. To help you, make up a form with these headings: *Brand name; Manufacturer; Weight; Size; Price; Price per pound or quart, etc.*

Compare the information you have gathered. Do some companies produce more than one brand? Is the price always related to the size and weight? What other factors might affect prices? Is there any way to compare the quality of different brands before you buy? Are ingredients listed on the package?

How is it useful to you as a consumer to compare brands in this way? How might it help you?

2. The growth of consumer law

Most consumer law cases begin as a dispute between a buyer and a seller. They come under civil law. In some cases, however, the state may believe a criminal law has been violated. It may then take the case to a criminal court.

For example, suppose the Johnsons order an expensive new television. Because of an error, the store delivers a less expensive one and the Johnsons refuse to pay. But the store's records show that the right TV was delivered. This dispute could end up in a court as a civil case.

Now suppose the store *deliberately* switched the TV sets. It is trying to obtain money by fraud. In this case a crime is involved.

Most consumer laws are quite recent. Until this century, there was no strong movement for consumer protection.

The first consumer laws dealt with the problem of false advertising. Interestingly, however, it was business, not the consumer, that pushed for laws against false advertising. Why? Because honest business people felt that they were losing out to dishonest ones.

For example, suppose two companies made sewing machines of about the same quality. One company advertised honestly that its machine could "sew some laces and light animal skins." The other company falsely claimed that its machine could "sew anything from the finest lace to the thickest hide." Many people would probably choose the dishonest company's machine.

To help fight this kind of unfair competition, an advertising magazine called *Printer's Ink* suggested a model law in 1911. The law said that anyone using untrue or misleading advertising would be guilty of a *misdemeanor*. This made false advertising a crime, not just a civil offense. Most states later adopted

some form of this law. But district attorneys found it took a lot of time to try to prove false advertising. So the law was never very effective. Still, it was a start.

In 1914 the federal government created the Federal Trade Commission (FTC). In its early years, however, the FTC worked mainly to protect businessmen from unfair competition.

In the 1940's, a group of lawyers started working out a set of laws on buying and selling. They hoped that these laws, known as the Uniform Commercial Code, would be accepted throughout the country. It took time, but today the Code is in use in nearly every state.

A part of the Code says that products sold by a merchant must be "fit for the . . . purposes for which such goods are sold." Suppose the seller knows that the buyer is depending upon him to select goods to meet a particular need. Then, the Code says, the seller is responsible for making sure that the goods will meet these needs.

By the time the Uniform Commercial Code was written, the FTC had also recognized the need for consumer protection. It began to sue businesses for unfair or dishonest treatment of consumers. Each case it won helped to strengthen consumer law.

Almost all of the laws protecting consumers today have come into being within the past 60 years.

3.
Protecting the consumer today

Since the early 1960's there has been a great rise in *consumerism*. This is a concern with helping the consumer in many different ways, from the safety of automobiles to the quality of packaged foods.

In recent years, many new consumer laws have been passed at all government levels. Let's look at some of the *federal* consumer laws.

A few years ago, you might get an unpleasant surprise when you bought a "jumbo" bag of potato chips. You could find that the size of the *bag* was jumbo, but it was less than half full. Today, the Fair Packaging and Labeling Act of 1969 protects you from that sort of problem. The true weight or volume of the contents must be clearly shown on the package. Misleading labels such as "jumbo" (when the weight or volume is not jumbo) may not be used.

In 1975 a Senate subcommittee checked 200 warranties from 51 companies. It found that most of them were not written clearly enough to inform consumers of all their rights under the warranties. As a result, a new federal law was passed. Today, it is illegal to make false statements on warranties or to leave out important information.

Still, there is no way the government can protect all consumer dealings. Our economy is just too big and complex for that. It is up to individual consumers to protect themselves.

Action Project

1. Report on a local law that protects consumers in your community.

2. Check the white pages of your telephone book to see whether you have a local Chamber of Commerce or Better Business Bureau. If so, invite a representative from one of these organizations to visit your classroom and discuss some of the ways in which they work to protect consumers' rights.

Chapter 2

Advertising and Consumer Protection

Advertising today is a multi-million-dollar industry. You find ads on highway billboards, in newspapers, magazines, and even paperback books. You see them in smoke up in the sky. And, of course, you hear them on the radio and see them on television.

Often advertising is the only source of information consumers have about a particular product or service. It may be the only way they can judge the qualities of things they plan to buy. Obviously, they cannot buy wisely if the claims made in ads are false or misleading.

Most business people are honest and believe that advertising should be honest, too. Yet in recent years there has been a great deal of criticism of advertising. This has come not only from consumer groups and government, but also from business itself. After all, if people find that some ads make false claims, they may be suspicious about others.

Today, it is against the law for

advertisers to make false or misleading claims. The Federal Trade Commision sets the rules for advertising and acts as watchdog. This is not always an easy job. As we will see, people can disagree on what is misleading or unfair.

1.
How to influence people

The main job of advertising, of course, is to influence buyers' choices of products and services. But the many different brands of one product may be very much alike. How do sellers persuade buyers to choose one particular brand? What kind of influence do they use in their ads?

First, they have to find out more about buyers and their choices. This is known as *market research.* Businesses spend millions of dollars each year to study the American buyer. Here are some of the questions they try to answer: Do people buy a product or service because they need it? Or are there sometimes other reasons? Do people buy for show? Do they buy because their friends do? Are they influenced by the packaging? Is there a demand for a new product or service? If not, can a demand be created?

Market researchers don't

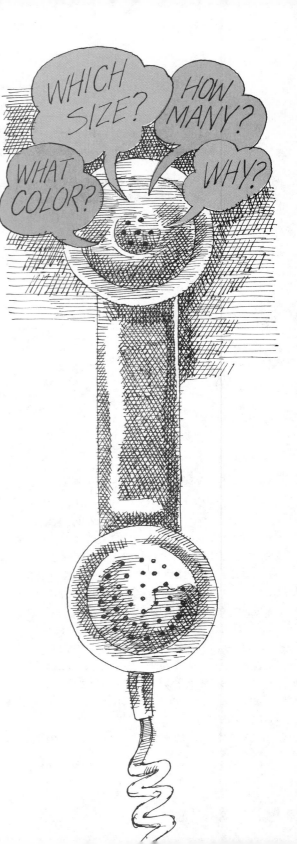

always find it easy to gather this information. They may have even more trouble knowing what to do with it. How do market researchers tackle these problems? You can get some idea from this interview with Joan M., who holds an important post with a large market research firm.

Interviewer: What kinds of businesses come to you for market research?

Joan: Most of our work is done for manufacturers and companies that provide services, such as airlines, and advertising agencies.

Interviewer: How do you get the information you need?

Joan: It depends upon the kind of information we're looking for. For example, we sometimes use the interview. We also conduct telephone polls. We research buying trends and patterns. And then there are more unusual methods.

Interviewer: What, for instance?

Joan: Well, market researchers may collect trash from a group of consumers and sift through it to find out what kinds of products they buy.

Interviewer: Do consumers always know when they're being tested?

Joan: No, they don't. When people know they're being tested, they may be self-conscious.

Interviewer: How do market researchers run tests that way?

Joan: Well, suppose they wanted to find out how people selected a brand of orange juice. They might set up a hidden movie camera in a supermarket, opposite the orange juice display. Later, they'd study the film to note people's expressions, how many cans were picked up before the final choice, things like that. Or suppose they wanted to find out how people bought hats or scarves. They might use a two-way mirror in a department store. Researchers would sit behind the mirror and make all kinds of notes. Do customers look at prices first or styles? Do they read cleaning instructions? How many hats or scarves do they try before making a decision?

Interviewer: If people knew they were being watched like that, wouldn't they object? Aren't you spying on them?

Joan: Not really. In a store, people know that clerks or guards may be watching them anyway. But I agree that this is a tricky subject.

An invasion of privacy?

Modern methods of gathering and using information raise some important questions about privacy. Do you have legal rights to personal privacy? If so, at what point are your rights invaded?

These questions go beyond advertising and market research. They also involve methods used by police and government agents for such purposes as crime detection and prevention. But the methods used in advertising and market research affect all citizens, not just those suspected of committing a crime.

In fact, one of the first cases involving rights of personal privacy had to do with advertising. In 1903, a New York woman named Roberson discovered that her picture was being used to advertise a brand of flour. So she sued the milling company. She lost the case because, at that time, there were no laws protecting personal privacy from such advertising practices. Shortly afterward, the state of New York passed one of the first personal privacy laws. This made it illegal to use information about a person to advertise a product unless the person gave permission. Soon, other states passed similar laws.

Today, the idea of personal privacy is recognized by law in most states. However, the law cannot tell you exactly where your rights of privacy begin and end. Often, it takes a court case to decide whether a particular invasion of privacy is illegal or not.

Your Turn

What advantages would people such as market researchers have in finding out about you without your knowing about it? What disadvantages might they have? Do you think there should be limits on the methods they can use to gather information about people while they are shopping and conducting their daily business? If so, what limits?

Field Activity

Conduct your own market research on the ways members of your class decide which brand of a particular product to buy. Agree upon one product, such as cereal, toothpaste, or soft drinks. Make a checklist of the qualities that describe that product. For example, with cereal you might describe appearance, taste, nutritive value, calorie content, box size, shape, color, and advertising. The next time you go to a supermarket, decide which brand of the product you would buy — though you need not actually buy it. Check off the qualities that affected your choice.

Compare your brand choice and selection process with those of other class members. Does a pattern emerge? Make a list of the reasons why people in your class tend to buy a particular product. What do you think are some ways that you, as a consumer, can protect yourself against "emotional" buying?

2.
Questionable advertising

As we have seen, advertising aims to inform *and* influence consumers. And market research can help advertisers find different ways of influencing people.

Some of these ways are straightforward. Others are not, and have been criticized as "questionable" or unfair. While they do not make false statements, they can create very misleading impressions.

Several questionable types of advertising are shown on the next few pages. Probably all of them are familiar to you.

The weasel

The weasel is known as an animal that is difficult to catch. A weasel in advertising is a word that is difficult to catch. It's there just to keep an ad from being false. See if you can find the weasel in the ad below:

The weasel is in the last sentence of the ad. If you take it out, the sentence reads, "Only Splash can give you clean washes!"

1. How does removing the weasel change the meaning of the sentence?

2. Is the statement true without the weasel? Why?

3. Is the statement true *with* the weasel? Why?

**"Dirty greasy grimy clothes? Try SPLASH!
Only SPLASH can give you clean SPLASH washes."**

"Scientific studies show that DYER BRAND DISINFECTANT kills germs."

False authority

In this type of ad, someone who looks like an expert makes claims about the quality of a product or service. It is illegal for an actor in commercials to say that he or she is a doctor, scientist, druggist, or teacher if it is not true. Still, it is possible to create that impression without actually saying it. Thus, a dignified person holding a medical book and talking about doctors' tests may be taken for a doctor.

1. Why would the advertiser wish to give the impression that a scientist is speaking?

2. Would the ad have the same effect if the person pictured were a plumber or a TV repairman? Why?

3. How successful do you think it is?

25

**"I owe my beautiful complexion to STAR LIGHT.
Why not do what the stars do?
Owe your beautiful complexion to STAR LIGHT."**

Celebrity testimonials

Some advertisers pay large sums of money to have a TV or sports star recommend their product or service. The reasons for this can be very complex. Perhaps the buyer remembers the ad better because he or she admires the celebrity. Perhaps the buyer respects the celebrity's opinion. If the celebrity is a glamorous personality, the buyer may feel that the product or service will put some glamour into his or her life.

Read the ad carefully again.

1. Why do you think advertisers might want a star like this to endorse their product?

2. What do you think is the purpose of this particular ad? How successful do you think it is?

Vague terms

Some ads *seem* to make big claims and promises. But when you examine them, they turn out to be so vague that they mean almost nothing. The ad below is a good example.

Read the ad carefully again. What is it actually saying?

1. Does the ad claim to keep you awake?

2. "Wake-up works fast." What is "fast"?

3. What does "fight tiredness" mean? Does the ad claim to win the fight?

4. What is the other product tested? Does the ad claim that it was a product that is supposed to keep you awake?

5. What do you think is the purpose of this ad? How effective do you think it is? Why?

"Want to stay awake? WAKE-UP works fast to fight tiredness. Twice as fast as other products tested."

Meaningless demonstrations

"Seeing is believing" is the principle upon which this type of ad is based. The demonstrations in many ads *can* be believed. But in others, you may not be seeing the entire picture. Take the ad above:

An average housewife explains that every day for the past month she has soaked her hands in "Bright 'N Clean" dishwashing liquid. She holds up her hands to show that her fingers are still soft, not cracked. "Bright 'N Clean" has not harmed her hands. Yet her dishes show that it really cleans.

The catch? Some dishwashing liquids do not begin to clean until they are mixed with hot water. The housewife in the ad above never claims to have soaked her hands in the same water used to wash the dishes. She may have soaked her hands in "Bright 'N Clean" and cold water. If so, the demonstration proves nothing. No mention is made of how much dishwashing liquid is in the soaking water. There may have been as little as a teaspoon of "Bright 'N Clean" to several gallons of water.

1. Why do you think advertisers sometimes use demonstrations like the one described above?

2. How effective do you think this kind of advertising is? Why?

Visual substitutions

Sometimes, to show a product on television or in a photo, a "look-alike" may be used. For example, whipped cream could melt under the hot lights of a photo studio. Or it might look too dull. So shaving cream might be used instead.

1. Why do you think advertisers might wish to substitute their product for one that is more photogenic?

2. Could this practice mislead consumers? If so, how?

Action Project

1. Make a study of ten different automobile advertisements. At least three of these should be television commercials. Keep a note pad handy when you watch TV and make a careful note of each commercial you choose. Look for the other automobile ads in newspapers and magazines. For each ad or commercial, write down: (a) how much *information* is given about the car; (b) what kind of *influence* is being used.

(For example, is the ad trying to convince you that the car is safe, or powerful, or showy, or inexpensive, or what?) Compare the different ads. Do some give much more information than others? If so, why? Is one kind of influence used more than others? If so, why? Are all of the ads and commercials aimed at the same kind of consumer? How can you tell?

2. Select one of the questionable advertising practices described in this section. Then choose a product or service you would like to advertise. Write an ad using the questionable advertising practice. Compare your ad with those written by other members of the class. Try to figure out what advertising practices they used in writing their ads.

3.
Advertising and the law

There is no law that states exactly what is fair advertising and what is not. In fact, it would be impossible to write such a law. The person writing it would have to know what new kinds of ads might be invented in the future.

Instead, there are many different laws that have something to say about fairness in advertising. How do they all fit together? This is where the Federal Trade Commission comes in. The FTC investigates complaints about false or deceptive advertising and makes a ruling in each case. If the ad is judged false or deceptive, the advertiser is ordered to stop using it.

Each new case adds to the total picture of advertising law. It makes the dividing line between what is legal and illegal just a bit clearer.

Anyone can write a letter to the FTC filing a complaint against a business. However, the FTC only handles cases which it considers to involve the "public interest." In other words, if you bought a box of cookies from a local bakery and didn't like the way they tasted, the FTC would not investigate the complaint. But if you complained that a nationwide department store chain was making false advertising claims, the FTC might well investigate.

When the FTC receives a complaint, it is first investigated by FTC staff members. If the staff decides that the ad violates a law, the FTC asks the company to stop the practice without admitting guilt. If the company does not stop or if it disagrees with staff findings, the FTC files a formal complaint. This leads to a public hearing before the five commissioners of the Federal Trade Commission.

If the FTC position is upheld, the company is ordered to stop the advertising practice. This is called an order to "cease and desist." If the company does not stop, it may have to pay large fines, sometimes as high as $10,000 a day.

Of course, companies do not always agree with Commission findings. If a company disagrees, it may take the case to a Court of Appeals. If the company is still dissatisfied, it may take the case to the Supreme Court.

Here is one case that was brought before the Commission. The staff of the FTC charged a company with breaking FTC rules in its advertising. And the Commission ordered the company to "cease and desist." The company appealed the FTC decision to the courts.

Tashof v. FTC

A company advertised eyeglasses at the low price of $7.50 each. The ad brought many customers in to buy. Yet of the 1,400 pairs of glasses sold, only 10 were sold at

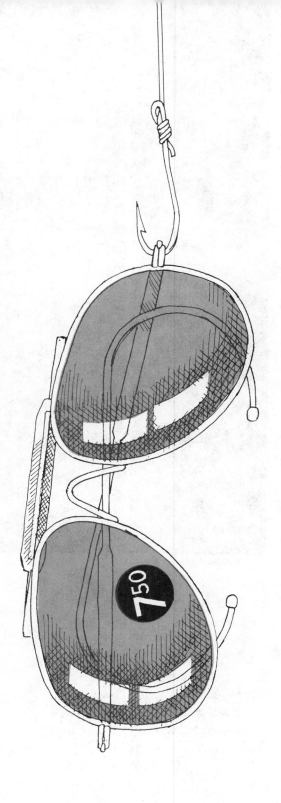

the sale price. The others were all more expensive models.

One of the buyers complained to the FTC. The FTC investigated and filed a formal complaint against the company. The FTC charged that the ad for $7.50 glasses was not honest. It charged that the ad was used to "bait" customers into the store for the purpose of "switching" them to more expensive glasses. In other words, the FTC said that the company never meant to sell the advertised glasses.

"Bait and switch" is a well-known deceptive advertising practice. Often the customer is told that all advertised stock has been sold or that the product isn't really very good. "Bait and switch" advertising is against FTC rules.

Tashof argued that the company did not use "bait and switch." It insisted that customers had not been deliberately switched from the advertised glasses. It claimed that most of them had just happened to choose more expensive models.

The FTC had no direct evidence of "bait and switch" advertising. It based its case on the numbers of eyeglasses at the different prices. It argued that the small number of advertised glasses sold (ten) indicated that, in fact, "bait and switch" had been used.

The Commission ruled against Tashof. Tashof disagreed with the decision and appealed the case to the U.S. Court of Appeals.

Your Turn

1. Do you agree that "bait and switch" is a deceptive advertising practice? Why?

2. If you were a judge hearing the case, would you agree with the FTC decision or with Tashof? For what reasons?

Your teacher can tell you the court decision in this case. It is on page 17 of the teaching guide.

Corrective advertising

A "cease and desist" order requires a company to stop doing whatever it is the FTC objects to. Recently, the FTC has gone still further in trying to protect consumers. In a few cases, it has demanded what is called *corrective advertising*. This means that the advertiser must not only stop the deceptive practice but must also tell the public that it *was* deceptive.

For example, a company advertised that its mouthwash would help prevent colds and relieve cold symptoms. The claims were false. When the FTC issued a "cease and desist" order, the company stopped the practice. But the FTC felt that, over the years, false ideas had been planted in consumers' minds. It therefore ordered corrective advertising. The company was told to present the following statement in all ads for the next two years:

"Contrary to prior advertising, Brand X will not prevent or cure colds or sore throats, and Brand X will not be beneficial in the treatment of cold symptoms or sore throats."

4.
Simulation: An FTC hearing

It is the December holiday season. The Apex Toy Company launches a nationwide campaign to promote its newest game. Here is how its television commercial goes:

A happy family is standing around a sturdy looking pool table with heavy legs. It is Sis's turn. She shoots the ball in the pocket. The family cheers. Then a voice speaks:

"Pool is a game the whole family can enjoy. So have your own professional-type pool table top. Made with the finest materials available, this top will probably last a lifetime. And it can be yours for only $199.95."

Across the country, thousands of these table tops are bought during the month of December. In January, a buyer complains to the FTC. The buyer makes two charges. First, he says that the pool table top is *not* of professional quality, as the commercial claims. Second, the $199.95 includes only the top, not the legs for the table or balls or cue sticks, as the commercial may suggest.

The FTC investigates the

complaint and decides that the commercial is misleading. The Apex Toy Company disagrees. It points out that the ad clearly says, " . . . have your own . . . pool table *top*. . . ." The ad never mentions anything about the legs or balls or cue sticks being included. Further, the company says, the commercial advertises a professional "type" table top, not a professional "quality" table top.

The FTC reasons that the commercial implies that everything shown is included in the purchase price. If those items are not included, it says, that fact should be mentioned in the commercial. Further, the FTC states that for a price of $199.95, the buyer has every reason to believe that he or she is paying for a professional-quality pool table rather than a toy.

The Apex Toy Company refuses to remove the commercial from the air. The FTC files a formal complaint and the case is scheduled for a hearing before the entire Commission.

1. Five members of the class should play the parts of the FTC commission will issue an order to members will play the parts of the attorneys representing the FTC and the Apex Toy Co., the official recorder, and individuals giving testimony for each side. The attorneys should study the outline of the case given above and prepare their arguments. The witnesses for the Apex Toy Company could include satisfied buyers and a storekeeper who sells all kinds of pool tables. Witnesses for the FTC could include dissatisfied buyers and another storekeeper. All witnesses should prepare stories about their experiences with the pool table top.

2. Conduct your own "FTC hearing" of the case. Seat the five commissioners at the front of the class. Facing them should be the attorneys and the official recorder. To start the hearing, the attorney for the FTC presents its side of the case. He or she then calls witnesses to support the FTC position. Then the attorney for the Apex Toy Co. presents *its* side of the case and calls witnesses. The commissioners can interrupt any time to ask questions. After both sides have been heard, the commissioners should meet and write a one-page report on their decision. If the firm is found guilty of misleading advertising, the Commission will issue an order to "cease and desist." If the Apex Toy Co. is found not guilty, the case will be dropped.

Chapter 3

Consumer Credit

"Will this be cash or charge?"

Today, you hear that question every time you go into a department store. More and more Americans are choosing credit rather than cash to pay for goods and services. For example, in 1950 consumer credit totaled $21.5 billion. By 1970 consumer credit was six times that amount — almost $127 billion. The use of consumer credit continues to rise.

What exactly is credit? In very simple terms, it is a promise to pay later for goods and services received now.

For example, if you buy a new color TV on credit, you don't have to wait to use the set until you've saved the hundreds of dollars it will cost. Instead, you have it now and pay for it a little at a time over a period of months or even years.

Some of the advantages of credit buying are obvious. It is convenient for buyers because they can use goods and services while paying for them. Payment terms can usually be worked out to fit the buyer's budget. Therefore, people can usually buy more with credit than they could afford with cash. And this, of course, benefits business.

However, credit buying must be

used carefully, for there are many dangers in using it. For one thing, it is expensive. You are paying not only for the item, but also for the credit. And credit buying can be too easy. People may run up huge monthly bills which they then find they cannot pay. The seller may then repossess (take back) the goods they bought and also sue them for the payments.

Still, when used wisely, credit can be a valuable tool for the consumer. And the more that people know about it, the better they can use it.

1.
Why not charge it?

Jeanie Johnston was feeling good. She had just finished a six-week training course and had gotten her first full-time job. She was now a secretary at a hospital.

Jeanie was on her way home from work. Something caught her eye in the window of Benson & Hart Department Store. There were the most beautiful boots she had ever seen.

"They're terrific," Jeanie thought. "But I won't have enough money until I get my first paycheck."

Jeanie spoke to Mr. Harmon, the head of the shoe department.

"Why don't you open a charge account with us?" Mr. Harmon asked. "Then you could buy the boots on credit."

"OK, I'll charge them," Jeanie said.

"Not so fast," Mr. Harmon said. "First you have to fill out a credit application. It'll take two or three days to process the application. Meantime, I'll hold the boots for you. If the application is approved, you come down and pick up the boots. Fair enough?"

"Fair enough!" Jeanie answered. Mr. Harmon gave her a credit application to fill out.

Application for Credit

BENSON AND HART DEPARTMENT STORE

Name of Applicant	Social Security Number	Driver's License
Address		How long
Previous Address (if within 5 years)		How long

Place of Employment	How long	Monthly Salary
Occupation		
Business Address		

Bank Account   -checking   -savings   -loan

Name of Bank	Branch	
Do you own your own home? yes no	Mortgage Holder	Monthly Mortgage	Purchase Price Balance

Credit References	Balance	Payments
1.		
2.		
3.		

Date   Signature of Applicant

Your Turn

1. Look at the credit application form on the previous page. What is meant by "Credit References," "Balance," and "Payments"? What do you think Jeanie put in these spaces?

2. What kind of information would a store want to have about applicants for credit?

A credit problem

For the next three days, Jeanie waited, hoping to hear from Benson & Hart. On the third day, she called the store to find out.

"Hello, this is Jeanie Johnston. I'm calling to find out whether my credit application has been approved."

"Just one moment please," said a voice on the other end of the line. After what seemed like a very long time, the voice spoke again. "I'm very sorry, Ms. Johnston, but Benson & Hart is unable to open a credit account for you at this time."

Jeanie was surprised. She felt embarrassed. All she could think to say was, "Thank you." Then she hung up the phone.

2. Who gets credit—and why

When you buy on credit, you promise to pay later for goods or services you receive now. No business will give credit unless it is reasonably sure that you will keep your promise to pay. How does a seller know whom to trust? Most sellers try to find out whether you have kept these kinds of promises in the past. If you have a good payment record, then you

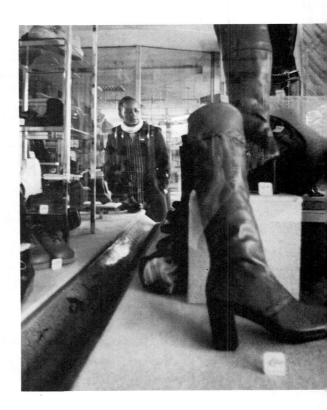

40

are probably a good credit risk.

Many businesses use the services of a credit reporting bureau to get or check this kind of information. A credit reporting bureau keeps records on people's debts and payments. For example, suppose you have credit accounts at two department stores. Then it is likely that a credit bureau has records of what you bought, what you paid, and how much money you still owe at each store. For a fee, businesses can look at these records. They can use the information to decide whether to give you credit.

How decisions are made

For several days Jeanie thought about her credit application. It bothered her that it had been turned down. At last she decided to speak to Mr. Harmon about it.

"Well of course, I'm very sorry," he said. "But there's nothing I can do about it. I don't make those decisions."

"But who does?" Jeanie asked.

"The credit department," Mr.

Harmon said. "It's right upstairs. Why don't you go and speak with them?"

Jeanie was a little nervous. She felt that the people in the credit office had decided she wasn't trustworthy. But she did want to know why her application had been turned down.

"May I help you?" asked a tall young woman about Jeanie's age.

"Yes," Jeanie said. "I applied for credit and was turned down. I'd like to know why."

"We base our decisions upon information we get from the credit bureau," the young woman replied.

Jeanie was surprised. "What was that information?" she asked.

"We can't tell you that. However, we will give you the name of the credit bureau. You can ask them."

That afternoon, Jeanie called the credit bureau. "Can I find out why my application was turned down?" she asked once again.

"We don't make credit decisions," the man on the phone said. "We only give information. However, if you would like to make an appointment to come down here, we'll be happy to show you what we have in your file."

3.
New credit laws

If Jeanie Johnston had applied for credit 10 years ago and been turned down, she might never have known why. Until recently, people had no legal right to know what was in their credit files. People were often refused credit because of items placed in their files by mistake. Without access to their files, people could not know about such errors and had no way to correct them.

All of this changed when the Fair Credit Reporting Act went into effect in 1971. This act protects consumers in many ways. For example, suppose you apply for credit and are turned down. You now have the right to:

1. know what is in your credit file;

2. have any information rechecked;

3. have incorrect or unproven information removed from your file;

4. place a statement in your file telling your side of any dispute.

This 1971 Act dealt only with information in credit files. It said nothing about other kinds of information, or the way that information was used. For example, a store might refuse credit simply because the customer was a single woman, or under 25. And it did not have to explain why.

This gap was filled by the Equal Credit Opportunity Act (ECOA), passed in 1974 and expanded in 1977. The new law makes it illegal for lenders to refuse credit for certain reasons. These include the applicant's sex, marital status, race, religion, and age (if old enough to apply legally for credit).

The Act goes further. It says that lenders must, if requested, give their reasons for refusing credit. They must also do this if they cancel or change the credit of a person who already has it.

Your Turn

1. Look at the reasons which, under the ECOA, *cannot* be used for refusing credit. Do you agree that all of these reasons should be barred? Why? What other reasons do you think might be barred by the law?

2. Jeanie went to the credit department at Benson & Hart to find out why she had been refused credit. Do you think the woman she spoke with met the requirements of the ECOA about providing information?

Looking at a credit record

The following week Jeanie made an appointment with the credit bureau. She took a long lunch hour and went to speak with Mr. Watson. He had her credit file out and waiting when she arrived.

Jeanie was stunned when she saw the report. "But there's nothing on it!" she said.

"That's right, Jeanie," said Mr. Watson. "You see, we only keep a record of your credit history. And you don't have any."

"But I thought Benson & Hart turned me down because there was something bad in my credit report."

"Well, I don't know why they turned you down," Mr. Watson answered. "But very often it is difficult to get credit without a credit record."

"But that's hopeless," Jeanie complained. "How can you get a credit record if nobody will give you credit the first time?"

Mr. Watson cleared his throat. "Getting credit the first time is not easy, but there are ways. Some stores have student cards or special accounts for young adults. These 'starter' accounts usually allow you a small credit limit, say fifty or seventy dollars."

"Are there other ways?"

"If you were in school, I'd suggest you take out a student loan. If you make your payments on time that's a good way to begin a credit rating. You could also try to finance a car. If you can't get financing by yourself, you might ask a family member to co-sign the loan with you."

"What does co-sign mean?" Jeanie asked.

Mr. Watson explained that a co-signer is someone who agrees to pay the loan if you fail to do so.

Jeanie thanked Mr. Watson for his time and walked slowly home. She had been saving money to buy a used car. Maybe she should put the money in a special account and ask her brother to co-sign the loan. On the other hand, it would cost more money to finance the car. As she walked, she tried to decide what to do.

Resource person. Find out what credit bureaus serve your area. Write a letter asking a representative from one of these agencies to visit your classroom. Decide in advance what questions you will ask. For example, you might want to find out about the best ways to establish a credit record in your community.

4.
What does credit cost?

Credit is convenient, but it costs money. The costs of credit are known as *finance charges* or *interest*. These charges can vary widely from business to business. Also the method of computing (working out) the charges can vary widely, too. Not surprisingly, credit users can get confused about finance charges. Until recently, there was no law which forced sellers to explain their interest rates to borrowers.

Suppose, for example, that 15 years ago a family bought an expensive stereo on credit. They agreed to pay $25 down and $10 a month until the total cost was covered. They might have been told that they were paying interest of, say, 1½ percent a month on the unpaid balance.

A rate of 1½ percent per month sounds quite low. But over a period of years, it can be very expensive. In fact, if the family took two or three years to work off the debt, they might have ended up paying as much as double the original price of the stereo. And they might never have been aware of the fact.

The Consumer Credit Protection Act of 1969 simplified things a bit. Often called the Truth-in-Lending Law, it requires sellers to tell buyers just what their credit costs. This information must include the annual percentage rate of the

SECURITY AGREEMENT AND DISCLOSURE STATEMENT

For value received, the borrower promises to pay to the order of Freeman Auto Sales, located at 1 Star Drive, Fairville, Ohio, **One thousand Forty-seven and no/100's** Dollars **($1047.00)** with interest at the rate of 14.00 per cent per year, payable as set forth below.

New or Used	Year Model	No. Cyl.	Make Trade Name	Model	Serial or I.D. Number	License
Used	**'74**	**4**	**Toyota**	**Cor. Sedan**	**R189016151**	_____

EQUIPPED WITH — Radio — Auto Trans. — Power Steering
ITEMS CHECKED — Heater — 4 Speed Trans. — Power Brakes

BORROWER	SELLER
Jeannine L. Johnston	**Freeman Auto Sales**
(Name)	(Name)
2121 S. Bend St.	**1 Star Drive**
(Street Address)	(Street Address)
Fairville, Ohio	**Fairville, Ohio**
(City & State)	(City & State)

1. AMOUNT FINANCED   **$1047.00**
2. FINANCE CHARGE   **$ 81.96**
3. ANNUAL PERCENTAGE RATE   **14.19%**
4. TOTAL PAYMENTS   **$1128.96**

Payable in **12** monthly installments of **94.08** each, beginning on **March 4, 1978** and continuing on the same date of each month until paid.

THE UNDERSIGNED ACKNOWLEDGES READING AND RECEIVING A LEGIBLE, COMPLETELY FILLED IN COPY OF THIS AGREEMENT AND CREDIT DISCLOSURE STATEMENT AND AGREES TO ITS TERMS AND CONDITIONS.

_____
(Signature of Borrower)

_____
(Signature of Co-Signer)

_____
(Date)

loan and the actual dollar charges.

Let's suppose for a moment that Jeanie Johnston did decide to buy a used car with her brother as co-signer. If she did, she would sign an agreement like the one on the previous page.

If you look at the lower left hand side of the contract, you will see that the price of the car is $1,047. And the finance charge that Jeanie must pay is $81.96. That amounts to 14 percent interest a year. This brings the total amount Jeanie will owe to $1,128.96. The terms are very clear. There is no confusion about how much the car is going to cost her.

The Truth-in-Lending Law does more than make the actual cost of credit clear. It also helps you to shop around for the best credit rates. Because rates differ widely, comparison shopping can be very important.

Also there are different types of credit which involve different methods of payment. And the way you pay for credit can affect the total cost. Let's look at two of the most common types of credit: *installment loans* and *revolving credit*.

Installment loans

When you borrow money from a bank or finance company, you usually must pay it back in monthly installments. You pay back more than you borrowed, because interest is added. However, as you will soon see, the loan actually costs you even *more* than this interest.

Suppose you take out a bank loan of $200 at 8 percent interest for one year. The interest charge is 8 percent of $200 or $16. So you have to pay back $216.

Now, if you paid this back in one lump at the end of the year, the total credit rate would also be 8 percent. But banks usually require you to start paying back within a few weeks, and pay off the whole loan by the end of the year. Suppose you start paying after one month. You only have the full use of the $200 for that first month. Then you make your first payment of $18 ($216 divided by 12). That means you now have the use of only $182. And after your second payment, you have only $164 — and so on.

By the end of the year, you will have nothing left of the $200. On the average during the year, you have had the use of only about *half* the money you borrowed. So your actual percentage rate was much more than 8 percent. In fact, it was about 16 percent.

Before the Truth-in-Lending

Law, most banks and finance companies would tell you only the basic interest rate (in this case, 8 percent). Now they must also tell you the *true annual percentage rate* (in this case, about 16 percent). Many people have found out for the first time what a loan really costs them.

Revolving credit

Many department stores, airlines, bank charge cards, and other businesses offer what is called revolving credit. A customer with a revolving charge account may charge anything up to a certain total. This total, known as the credit limit, is often from $100 to $500. If the customer pays the entire amount which is owed within 30 days, there is usually no interest charge. However, the customer only *has* to pay a portion of the amount owing. Then finance charges are added each month until the account is paid in full. In most cases, the customer goes on borrowing and repaying again and again. Money keeps going into and out of the account — which is why it is called *revolving*.

Your Turn

1. Joe borrows $300 for a year at 9 percent basic interest. He has to pay back $327 in 12 monthly installments of $27.25 each. About how much of the loan does he actually get to use during the year? What, roughly, is the true annual percentage rate?

2. In shopping around for a loan, what other factors should you consider besides the interest rate?

Credit in court

What happens if a lender does *not* give the information required by the Truth-in-Lending Law? The borrower can then take the lender to court. If the borrower wins the case, the lender may have to pay twice the amount of the finance charge. The lender will also have to pay court costs and lawyers' fees.

As an example, let's go back to Jeanie Johnston and her car (see page 44). Suppose the auto dealer had told her she could take a year to pay for the car and it would cost her $1128.96. The written agreement said nothing about the basic cost of the car or the finance charge. By law, this information must be given to the borrower.

If she wanted, Jeanie could sue the dealer. And if she proved her case, the dealer would have to pay her $163.92, which is twice the finance charge.

Chapter 4

Protecting Yourself as Consumer

Alan is in a hurry. He needs some new floor mats for his car and his date is expecting him in 15 minutes. He stops at an automotive supply store and picks up the first set of mats he sees. He taps his foot on the floor as he waits in line to pay.

"That will be $12.50, sir," the salesman says.

Alan pulls out the cash and hands it to the salesman. He picks up the floor mats and starts toward the door.

"Wouldn't you like me to wrap them? How about your receipt?" the salesman calls after him.

"Forget it!" Alan shouts. "I don't have time!"

1. The consumer: careless or informed?

Unfortunately, too many people buy things the way Alan did. To begin with, Alan didn't stop to choose. He didn't check that the floor mats were the size, color, or quality he really wanted. Later, he might want to exchange them. But if so, he could have trouble proving he had bought the mats at that store because he didn't wait for a receipt.

If Alan ends up losing money on the deal, he has no one else to blame. He cheated himself.

The best way to protect yourself

is to become an informed consumer. Before deciding to buy anything, make sure you know what you *want* and what you are likely to *get*. Here are some basic questions you should ask yourself:

- Is this something I really need or want? Why?
- How does it compare with other similar products or services?
- What do I expect from the product or service? Am I expecting too much?
- How long can I expect this product or service to last? Is this satisfactory?
- Is it worth the cost?
- Can I afford it?

Suppose you answer these questions and decide that you still want to buy. As an informed consumer, you will take several more steps before you finally make the purchase. Some of these steps are described on the following pages.

Are you making the right choice?

Shop around before you buy. Compare values and prices. Gather as much information as you need to make an informed choice. If it is an important purchase, check a buying guide. For example, some guides for consumers compare auto makes in detail. They list prices and point out the strengths and weaknesses of different models.

Is it guaranteed?

Check guarantees (also known as warranties) carefully before you buy. Know what they do and do not promise. Compare guarantees of different brands. For example, one clock radio might be guaranteed for breakdowns only for 30 days, while another is covered for 90 days or even a year. The guarantee may show what the seller thinks of the quality of the product or service.

Can you return it?

Before you buy, ask about the store policy on returning or exchanging goods. Be especially careful about items marked "sale" or "as is." Many stores will not accept these items for return or exchange. In this case, the sale is called "final." Remember you can shop around to find better return or exchange policies. Often, large department stores have more liberal policies than small neighborhood stores.

How do you have to pay?

Don't agree to pay more than you can afford. If you put something on lay-away, know exactly what

49

the conditions are. Find out how large the deposit must be, the conditions of payment, and the time allowed. Find out about refund policies if you change your mind or are unable to complete the payments.

Your Turn

Here are three different buying problems that you might run into. What would you do in each case? Discuss the problems with the rest of the class and compare your decisions.

1. A coat you have been admiring for many months is on sale. You need a coat but you don't have enough money to buy it right now. There is a good chance that you will have enough within the next 60 days. What would you do?

2. You see an FM radio on sale. It is exactly the kind you want to buy and the salesman tells you it is the last one in the store. He tells you that you won't be able to find it at a better price. You are not sure. This is the first store you have gone to. You might be able to buy it at a better price somewhere else. Still, it seems like a good buy and if you wait, it might be gone. What would you do?

3. You have been saving your money for three months to buy a tape deck. You have the model picked out and have saved almost enough money to get it. On an impulse, you stop at another store. You see another brand of tape deck. It isn't exactly what you want and the guarantee is not as good. But it's a lot cheaper. In fact, you have enough money to buy it right now. What would you do?

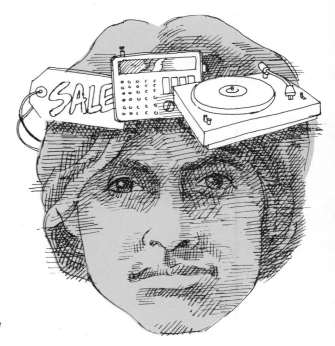

2.
If you have a consumer complaint

By following the tips in the previous section you can avoid a lot of problems. Still, even the most careful buyer will sometimes run into trouble. For example, a store may deliver a wrong or broken item. You may be kept waiting for a guaranteed repair. Or a store may bill you in error for a payment you have already made. In cases like these, you need to make a complaint.

How do you go about making complaints? In the following interview, James Borman, a consumer affairs specialist, describes some of the steps you can take.

Interviewer: What's the first thing you should do when you have a consumer complaint?

Borman: The first thing is to contact the store where the purchase was made.

Interviewer: What person at the store should you talk to?

Borman: It's best to start with the salesperson who sold you the item. If that doesn't work, ask to speak with the manager.

Interviewer: What should you say and do?

Borman: Well, let's first see what you *shouldn't* say and do. You shouldn't storm in, make a scene, and start yelling threats. This kind of behavior doesn't usually solve the problem. What you *should* do is to be firm, clear, and polite. Explain the problem and say what you want the store to do to correct it. You should also have with you any papers relating to the complaint — sales slips, guarantees, and so forth.

Interviewer: What if talking to the salesperson and the manager doesn't work?

Borman: Then write a letter to the owner of the business, or the sales representative of the company that makes the items, or even to the president of the company. Again, it's important to be polite, firm, and very clear about how you want your complaint handled.

Interviewer: How effective are these methods?

Borman: Very often they are enough to clear up the problem. Most businesses want to please their customers and will do what they can to make sure that you're satisfied. In fact, many companies have consumer complaint departments for that purpose.

Interviewer: Suppose none of

these things work. Is there anything else you can do?

Borman: Yes. You can file a complaint with a local agency or organization which deals with consumer problems. For example, many local Better Business Bureaus and Chambers of Commerce try to help solve consumer complaints. Or if there is a Consumer Affairs column in your local paper, you can write a letter to the editor explaining your problem. Also, many local radio and TV stations have consumer action programs where they explain your problem on the air. This often brings very quick results.

Interviewer: What if none of these steps work?

Borman: Then there are state agencies you can contact, as well as federal agencies and consumer advocate organizations. As a last resort, you can take legal action.

Interviewer: If you can just refer a consumer complaint to someone else, why bother to try and solve it yourself?

Borman: Because in most cases you will save yourself a lot of time and sometimes money. As I said, a complaint to the store or company usually gets quick results. Most consumer protection agencies are overloaded with complaints, so it may take months before they can deal with yours.

Interviewer: So could you sum up your advice to dissatisfied consumers?

Borman: Certainly. First complain to the seller. If that fails, contact the manufacturer. And if that fails, by all means refer your complaint to one of the agencies suggested, starting at the local level.

Interviewer: Any final advice?

Borman: Yes — and this is most important. Whatever you do, if you have a consumer complaint, complain. Don't just let it go. If you do nothing, you're hurting yourself as well as every other consumer.

Action Project

Find out what local agencies and organizations deal with consumer problems in your area. You can look them up in the white pages of your telephone book. Check under city, county, and state offices as well as under consumer offices.

Invite representatives from one of the organizations to visit your classroom, or arrange a field trip to one of their offices. Think about the kind of information you would like to have. Then prepare a list of interview questions.

3.
Your day in court

If you cannot settle a consumer complaint any other way, you may decide to take legal action. Hiring a lawyer and filing a lawsuit can be very expensive. In fact, these may cost a lot more than the money you hope to get back from your complaints. However, many states have an inexpensive way for consumers to take legal action. This is a special court usually known as Small Claims Court.

You can file a suit in a Small Claims Court if someone owes you money. There are limits on the amount of money that can be won in a Small Claims Court. For example, in California the limit is $750, in New Mexico $2,000, and in Ohio $150.

Small Claims Court has many advantages. It is run on simple lines, without difficult legal terms. In some states, you may be represented by a lawyer if you wish. In other states, such as Michigan, Oregon, and Idaho,

lawyers are not permitted. Filing a suit is inexpensive. Court costs usually run about five dollars.

Usually you can file a suit in a Small Claims Court if you are older than 18. If you are younger, an adult must go with you when you file a suit. In some states you must be 21 or older.

Suppose you have a case that you want heard in Small Claims Court. You sold an old ten-speed bicycle to Roy, a friend of a neighbor. Roy agreed to pay you $25 within two weeks. The first day he had the bike, he left it parked in front of the library. Someone stole it. Now he refuses to pay you.

You have already filed your suit and paid a small filing fee. Roy has been served an order to appear and a court date has been set. You have a witness who was with you when Roy bought the bike. That witness will testify in court that Roy agreed to pay you $25 for the bike. You also have an agreement Roy signed promising to pay you the $25 within two weeks for the sale.

There was another witness to the sale, the neighbor who is Roy's friend. You asked him to testify but he refused. You could ask the court clerk to issue a "subpoena" to this person. Then

he would have to appear. But you decide that you have enough evidence to win your case without him.

Trial day

The day of the trial arrives. You go to the court building a little early. You ask the clerk where your case will be heard. You check the courtroom calendar to make sure that your case is listed. It's there all right.

You take a seat inside the courtroom and wait for the judge to enter. After he has been seated, he explains the Small Claims Court procedures. You're feeling a little nervous now.

The court clerk announces your case. You and your witness and Roy all come forward to take an oath that you will tell the truth.

It's your turn first. You tell the judge what happened. You hand him the paper of agreement. The judge doesn't ask you or your witness any questions. You feel that you have presented your case well.

Now it is Roy's turn. He explains that it doesn't seem fair to have to pay you for a bike that has been stolen. The judge asks whether Roy agreed to pay you $25 and whether that is his signature on the agreement note. Roy admits to both.

The decision

It does not take the judge long to make up his mind. He decides the case in your favor and orders Roy to pay you the $25 plus the court costs. You are told that the court clerk will help you collect the money if you have any problem.

Roy gives you the $25 and you are feeling pretty good about the whole thing. If you ever have to go to Small Claims Court again you will know just what to expect and how to prepare.

Field Activity

Call your local county courthouse to find out whether there is a Small Claims Court in your area. If there is, arrange to visit the court in session. During your visit, note the kinds of cases heard. Also note the roles played by the presiding judge, the court clerk, the plaintiff (the person filing suit), the defendant (the person against whom the suit has been filed), and the witnesses for both. Pay close attention to the kinds of evidence presented and to the decisions handed down by the judge.

4. Simulation: Small Claims Court

Assign various members of the class to play the roles of the plaintiff(s), defendant(s), and witnesses in each of the cases described below.

Plaintiffs, defendants, and witnesses should read the facts of their case and decide what they will say in court.

Invite a local attorney or judge to visit your class and play the part of the presiding judge in your Small Claims Court simulation. If this cannot be arranged, choose a student to be the judge. Also choose a student to play the court clerk.

Case No. 1: *Russell v. Royal Dry Cleaners*

Janet Russell took a $40 silk blouse to the Royal Dry Cleaners to have it cleaned. She had worn it only once. When she picked it up, it had an ink stain about the size of a dime near the collar. Janet said that the stain was not there when she brought the blouse in. A friend who came with her when she first brought the blouse in agreed that it had no stains. Janet asked that the dry cleaners pay her the $40 the blouse cost. She had the receipt to prove she had paid $40 for it. Royal Dry Cleaners denied that it was responsible for the spot. It also argued that, in any case, the blouse was used clothing and no longer worth $40. Janet argued that it would cost her at least $40 to replace it.

Case No. 2: *Lou's Automotive v. Drainer*

Harold Drainer took his '77 Chevrolet station wagon to Lou's Automotive to have a faulty ignition switch repaired. Lou's Automotive filled out a work order which Mr. Drainer signed. That night he picked up his car, and the ignition switch seemed to be fine. He paid for the work with a check. The next morning when he got into his car, the ignition switch did not work at all. He called Lou's Automotive to complain. They insisted that the repairs had been properly made and that he must have damaged the switch himself. Mr. Drainer went to his bank and stopped payment on the check he had written to Lou's Automotive. He then called in another car repair company to fix the ignition switch. Lou's Automotive took him to Small Claims Court to collect the money owing on the repairs they had made.

Hearings and decisions

If possible, the hearing of each case should follow the same procedure used in a real Small Claims Court. You can be guided by the visiting judge or attorney, or by your own visit to a court.

After hearing each case, the judge will make a decision, which may include a money award.

Following the simulation, the class should discuss the various decisions. In each case, the judge should give reasons for the decision so that these too can be discussed.

Consumer Law: a Bibliography

Law and the Consumer
*by Robert Berger and Joseph
Teplin, Houghton Mifflin, 1969.*
Deals with advertising, credit, and
consumer protection.

The Consumer
*edited by Gerald Leinwand,
Pocket Books, 1970.*
Covers consumer problems and
self-protection.

Buyers Beware
Scott, Foresman, 1969.
Deals with advertising,
comparative shopping, and
consumer law.

**Buy It Right; An Introduction
to Consumerism**
*by Jean Embe and Clifford Earl,
E. P. Dutton & Co., 1974.*
Guide to wise consumerism,
including use of credit.

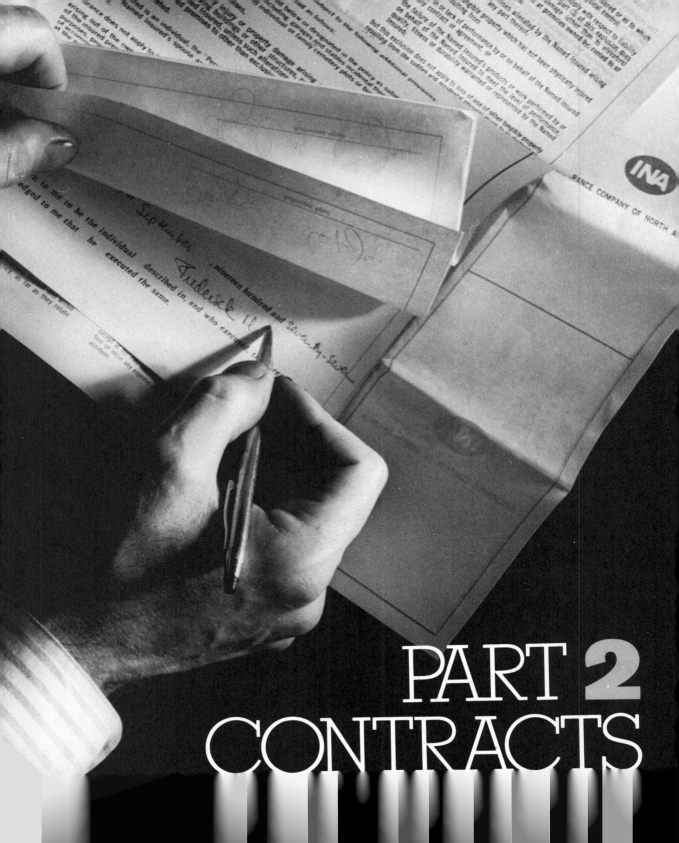

PART 2
CONTRACTS

Chapter 5

What Is a Contract ?

"I'll give you twenty dollars for that saw!"

"Done!"

"Only $1.50 a week for two quarts of milk delivered to my home? Sounds good. I'll take it."

"If you let me have all the peaches I can pick from your tree today, I'll mow your lawn every week for a month."

"You're on!"

What do those three short scenes have in common? They are all examples of contracts. A contract is a promise that is backed by the law.

The buyer promises to pay $20 for the saw and the seller agrees. Under the law, both the buyer and the seller must now carry out their agreement.

The dairy promises to deliver two quarts of milk a week to the customer's home. The customer *accepts and must pay $1.50 a week in return for the service.*

A teenager promises to mow the lawn every week for a month in return for fresh peaches. The neighbor agrees. The lawn must be mowed and the peaches must be given.

As you can see, a contract doesn't always have to be written down. There don't have to be lawyers around. There don't even have to be any witnesses. All a contract takes is two parties — that is, two people who make a special agreement.

Is any promise a contract? Can you make contracts even if you are under 18? What happens if you have second thoughts about a contract? What can you do if someone breaks a contract with you? These are some of the questions we will explore in this unit.

1.
Agreements and the law

A contract is an agreement that usually involves money, goods, or services. Like the three examples above, most contracts in everyday life are simple. They don't involve a lot of money, and often nobody minds too much if the contract is broken.

A friend offers to swap a record album with you, and you agree. Later, the friend calls you and says he's changed his mind. Maybe you're a bit annoyed, but you just shrug your shoulders. You don't think of calling a lawyer.

Still, even simple contracts are backed by the law. And each party can insist that the contract be kept. For example:

You offer a neighbor $25 for his old CB radio. He accepts your offer. You give him $5 and go home to get the rest of the money. When you return, the man says he wants to sell the CB to someone else who will pay $50 for it.

The contract you have made with the neighbor protects you. Since he agreed to sell the CB to you, he cannot just change his mind. If he does, you have the right to take legal action.

Field Activity

Make a list of all of the agreements you observe or take part in during any one day. Write these headings on a piece of paper: Location (where the contract was made); Description; Parties (the people making the contract). For example: "Drugstore. Someone orders a milk shake (that is, promises to pay for it). Customer and drugstore clerk."

Look at the examples of contracts on page 59 and compare them with the agreements you have listed. Which of the agreements on your list do you think are legal contracts? Put a check mark against each of these.

2.
What makes a promise a contract?

Do all promises form contracts? No — only some do. In both stories below, a promise is given. But one of the promises becomes a contract while the other does not. See if you can tell which is which.

Story No. 1

Larry is excited. "We're moving to the west coast," he tells his best friend Jerry. "I can't take a lot of stuff with me so I'll give you my record collection."

"I accept," Jerry says happily. He is sorry Larry is leaving but there are some great LPs in the collection.

"By the way," Larry adds, "do you think you can come by on Saturday and help me pack? You can pick up the records then."

"Sure thing," Jerry answers. "And thanks, Larry."

Story No. 2

Larry is excited. "We're moving to the west coast," he tells his best friend Jerry. "I can't take a lot of stuff with me so I'll give you my record collection if you'll come over and help me pack on Saturday."

"I accept," Jerry says happily. "And thanks, Larry."

Which of the two stories do you think contains the contract? Why?

Story No. 2 is the one with the contract. In both stories, Larry offers Jerry his record collection and asks Jerry to help him pack. But only in No. 2 does Larry ask Jerry to help him pack *in return for* the records. When Jerry accepts this offer, there is a contract.

In most cases, a contract must contain three things:
- an offer;
- acceptance;
- consideration (something in return).

On the following pages we will find out more about each of these.

The offer

An offer is a promise to do something in exchange for something else.

"I'll give you my record collection," is not an offer. No exchange is involved. In Story No. 1, Larry simply makes a gift of his records. He asks Jerry to help him pack and Jerry agrees. But that is not a condition of the gift. Larry says he will give the records to Jerry whether he helps pack or not. So there is no legal obligation on either of them. Larry can change his mind and keep the records — even if Jerry helps him pack. Or Jerry can accept the records even if he does not help with the packing.

"I'll give you my record collection if you help me pack," is more than a promise. In Story No. 2, Larry promises to give Jerry the records only *in exchange for* Jerry's help. This is an offer. When Jerry accepts it, a contract is made. If Jerry helps him pack, Larry has a legal obligation to give him the record collection as promised.

Suppose Larry had said to Jerry, "Maybe I should give my record collection to someone in return for helping me pack. If I decide to do that, would you be interested?" Would that be an offer? No. If Jerry said "Yes," Larry could still change his mind and not make the offer. To create a contract, an

offer must be definite.

Now suppose Sally offers to sell Karen her bike for $15 and Karen says she wants to think it over. Sally also thinks it over and phones Karen that evening.

"Sorry, Karen, but I've decided not to sell my bike after all."

"That's too bad!" says Karen. "I'd just make up my mind to buy it."

But Karen is too late. Sally has withdrawn her offer, and it no longer holds good. An offer can be withdrawn any time before it is accepted.

Suppose Karen had called first, accepting the offer. In that case, it would be too late for Sally to change her mind. Once an offer is accepted, it can no longer be withdrawn.

An offer may include a time limit. Sally could have said: "I'll sell you my bike for $15. But you have to let me know by eight o'clock this evening." If Karen doesn't call until five past eight, the offer no longer stands.

Your Turn

Look at each of the examples of offers given below. Decide which of these offers could form a contract if accepted and which could not.

1. Mr. Jones says to Mr. Brown, "I will sell you all the tools in my garage for $200."

2. Janice says to Lois, "I've been thinking about selling my skis. If I decide to sell them for $25, would you be interested in buying them?

3. Marilyn says to David, "I'm going to give you my old geometry book. Will you take it?"

4. Mrs. Arliss says to Lois, "I'll pay you $2 an hour to weed my garden."

Look again at each of the offers which could *not* form a contract if accepted. What changes would turn them into contractual offers?

The acceptance

When there is an offer, it must be accepted as is to make a contract. In other words, the offer must be accepted on all its terms. For example:

Mary Ellen receives a letter in the mail. The letter reads:

I will sell you my goat for $30. Let me know if you wish to buy it.

Mary Ellen decides to buy the goat and writes immediately to say so. She accepts the offer as is and a contract is made. The owner must sell the goat for $30 and Mary Ellen must buy it for that amount.

Suppose Mary Ellen had answered the letter differently, like this:

I like the goat and will pay you $30 but I want a month's feed thrown in too for that price. Enclosed is my check for $30.

Would there be a contract? No, because now Mary Ellen does *not* accept the offer as is. An offer cannot be accepted in part. It must be accepted exactly as is or else it is rejected.

Mary Ellen is making what is called a "counter-offer." This creates a new contract situation, one in which Mary Ellen makes the offer. She is offering $30 for the goat and a month's worth of feed. It is now up to the owner to decide whether to accept *her* offer.

Meeting all conditions

An offer may contain various conditions. It may say how soon an answer must be given, or how soon payment must be made. A person accepting the offer must also accept all of these conditions, or else the offer is rejected. For example:

Suppose the owner of the goat had said, "If you wish to accept my offer, you must be at my farm in person at 3:00 p.m. on Tuesday, November 14th with $30 in cash." Mary Ellen would have had to follow all of these terms. If not, she would have rejected the offer.

However, suppose the goat owner had simply asked Mary Ellen to let him know by return mail. In that case, she could probably reply by any equally quick (or quicker) means. It would probably be all right for her to telephone her acceptance or to go directly to the goat owner's home.

Your Turn

Look at each of the examples of acceptances given below. Decide which of these would create a contract and which would not.

1. Janice sends a telegram which reads, "As you requested, I am cabling my acceptance of your offer. I agree to pay $75 for your freezer."

2. Ms. Smith offers to sell Mr. Willis an interest in her land if he accepts in person at her office by 10:00 a.m. Thursday. Instead, Mr. Willis mails a letter of acceptance late Wednesday evening.

3. Louise says to Anna, "Yes, I agree to help you with your math in return for a dinner at 'Le Gourmet' — but I wonder if you'd consider throwing in that brown dress you don't wear anymore, too?"

4. Mrs. Wandaman asks Mr. Jones to let her know by return mail whether he accepts her offer to sell her sofa. Mr. Jones sends a messenger with an acceptance

and a check as soon as the offer is received.

Look again at those acceptances which do not lead to a contract. Why not? What changes would make them lead to a contract?

The consideration

We have seen that an offer is a promise to do something in exchange for something else. This "something else" is known as *consideration*. After an offer is accepted, consideration must be given or there is no contract.

Consideration may be money, goods, work, or some other action. But the person accepting the offer must, now or later, give or do *something* of value. Otherwise the person making the offer does not legally have to keep his or her promise.

Some examples will make this clear. When Mary Ellen accepted the offer of a goat, the consideration was money—$30 which she paid later. When Jerry accepted Larry's offer of the record collection, the consideration was work—helping Larry to pack on the following Saturday.

Here's another example. Mrs. James says to her 16-year-old son, "You are old enough to have a driver's license. But I'd feel happier if you didn't drive until you are older. I will buy you a car when you are 21 if you don't drive until that time." Her son accepts and does not drive for five years. Is his mother legally bound to give him a car? Is there a contract?

Yes. The consideration is the son's action of *not* driving. This is something of value to his mother. It is also something he can choose not to give if he does not wish to.

The person accepting the offer must be able to choose whether or not to give the consideration. If there's no choice, there's no contract. For example:

Suppose Mrs. James says, "Son, you are now 16 years old. Because of the help you've given me over the years with the other children, I'm going to give you a car."

Mrs. James would be offering her son a gift in return for something he had already done. There is nothing now he can choose to give or not give. So there is no legal contract.

Now suppose the person to whom the promise is made has to give the consideration anyway. Again, there is no choice and no contract. For example:

Suppose Mrs. James puts her offer a little differently. She says, "Son, if you obey the

traffic rules and don't get any tickets until you are 21, I will buy you a new car on your 21st birthday."

In this case, Mrs. James is asking for something her son already has to do under the law. With or without her promise, he must obey traffic rules, so Mrs. James would *not* be legally obligated to buy him a car.

Your Turn

Here are some examples of offers. Look at the consideration involved in each. On the basis of what you have just read, decide which offers could make a legal contract and which could not.

1. Don says to Anna, "I will pay you $3 if you will take my car to the car wash before five this afternoon." Anna agrees.

2. Mrs. Williams says to Lois, "Because you have such a nice voice, I promise you will be the one to sing a solo at graduation."

3. Mr. Grant says to his daughter, "If you promise not to drink alcohol until you are legally of age, I will send you on a trip to Europe for your 21st birthday."

4. Mrs. Moore says to Lewis, "You've always done a good job on the lawn, so if you mow it for me before 3:00 p.m. today I'll give you $5."

Look again at those examples which have the wrong kind of consideration for a contract. What changes would make them the right kind?

3.
Is there a contract?

Each of the following is an actual contract case. Read each to decide whether you think a legal contract does or does not exist. Remember, a contract must contain:

1. a definite offer;
2. unconditional acceptance;
3. the right kind of consideration.

Scott v. People's Monthly

People's Monthly, a magazine, announced a "Word Building Contest." The contest offered a first prize of $1,000 to the person who created the largest list of words from the letters in "determination."

A list of rules went with the contest offer. Contestants could not use certain kinds of words, such as abbreviations.

Mrs. Scott sent in the longest list of words. Yet she did not win the contest or the $1,000 prize. She took *People's Monthly* to court. She argued that she created the longest list and was therefore entitled to the first prize.

People's Monthly agreed Mrs. Scott's list was longest. However, it pointed out that some of her words fell within the word types

prohibited by contest rules. It therefore argued that she was not entitled to the first prize.

Your Turn

1. Do you think a contract exists in this case? Why?

2. If you were deciding the case, would you decide in favor of Mrs. Scott or *People's Monthly*? Why?

Hamer v. Sidway

A wealthy man promised to pay his nephew $5,000 if he did not smoke or drink until he was 21. The nephew agreed. Although he was legally entitled to smoke and drink, he did not do so until he was 21. Then he asked his uncle for the $5,000 promised. The uncle refused to pay. The nephew sued.

The uncle argued that his nephew had not exchanged anything of value in return for the promise. In fact, he claimed that the nephew had actually gained a benefit by not smoking or drinking. That meant there was no consideration and therefore no contract.

The nephew disagreed. He argued that he *had* given up something of value in return for the promise of $5,000. This "something" was his legal right to smoke and drink.

Your Turn

Do you think a contract exists? If you were a judge, how would you rule?

Your teacher can tell you the decisions in these cases. They are on page 24 of the Teaching Guide.

Another look

Now that you know more about what makes a contract, look at the list of agreements you were asked to make on page 60. Check your examples carefully. Which of them actually include offer, acceptance, and consideration? Which do not? Strike out those agreements which you do not consider to be legal contracts.

4.
Written contracts

All contracts *may* be put in writing, but most are legal even if they are not written down. In our daily lives, contracts are usually spoken. A pizza parlor would lose time and business if it asked its customers to put their orders in writing.

However, certain kinds of contracts *must* be in writing. As we will see, there are good reasons for this.

Before the late 1600's there were no laws in England or the American colonies requiring written contracts. So people could claim that they were parties to contracts which did not exist, and there was often no way to prove them wrong. These claims could involve large amounts of money or land. They could cause a lot of trouble to many people.

In 1677 the English Parliament passed a law known as the Statute of Frauds. This statute is the basis of many of our state laws today. Under these laws, no legal action can be taken on certain contracts unless the parties have signed a written agreement.

What kinds of contracts must be in writing? Usually, those that involve large amounts of money or goods. For example, in most states a contract must be in writing if it involves:
• the sale of goods worth more than a certain amount (usually from $50 to $500, depending on the state); or
• the sale of real estate.

In addition, contracts with certain complicated terms must be in writing. These usually include contracts which:
• cannot be completed in less than one year;
• promise to pay the debt of another person.

What kind of contract is needed?

Read the stories below and decide in each case whether a spoken or written contract is best. Keep in mind that contracts which fall under the Statute of Frauds must be in writing. In the other cases, decide for yourself which kind of contract is more convenient.

1. Dave offers to sell his motor bike to Jim for $100. Dave says the bike is in excellent condition and just needs a tune-up. Jim accepts the offer on the strength of Dave's assurance that the motor bike really is in excellent condition.

2. Mr. and Mrs. Novak contract with a landscape architect, Mr. Davidson, to turn their backyard into a flower garden. They agree to pay him for all the materials he uses plus a fee of $2400. Davidson explains that because of the changing seasons, he will have to plant the different flowers over a period of time. He estimates that the entire landscaping work will take about 15 months.

3. Juan has wanted a purebred German Shepherd for a long time. He sees an ad in the paper offering pure German Shepherd puppies for sale at $30 each. He goes to look at the puppies and finds one he wants to buy. He offers the owner, Roger, $25 for the puppy. Roger accepts the offer.

4. Joyce wants to buy a car from a neighbor. She doesn't have enough cash and wants him to let her pay the $500 at the rate of $60 per month. The neighbor is willing, but wants her father or mother to agree to pay off the car if Joyce fails to do so. Joyce's mother says she will make that agreement.

Action Project

As a class activity, make a list of the situations which must be covered by a written contract. Add any other situations which you think *should* be in writing. Then divide into groups. Have each group choose one of the situations and work out a specific contract. To do this, group members should assume the roles of various parties to the contract. The group should then attempt to agree upon and write a clear, foolproof contract.

As a guide, make sure that each contract includes:
• the names of the contracting parties;
• the purpose of the contract;
• the consideration;
• the date of agreement;
• signatures of all parties.

Chapter 6

Contracts in Court

You have just made a contract with someone. As far as you know, it is a legal contract—it fits the requirements listed in Chapter Five.

Suppose you now have second thoughts about the contract. Or circumstances have changed, and you cannot meet your part of the bargain. Are you stuck with the contract or can you get out of it?

Or suppose the other party has second thoughts and decides to break the contract. But you want the contract to continue. Can you do anything about it? If so, what?

This chapter takes a look at some of the problems that can arise after a contract has been made. And it shows how the law deals with these problems.

1.
Minors and contracts

Joanna is 17. All her life she has wanted to be a fashion model. One day on the way home from her summer job at a neighborhood store she sees a notice on a door. The notice reads:

Enter the world of high fashion. Make top dollars as a fashion model. If you have what it takes, step through this door. Our agency may change your life.

Joanna pauses for a moment. Does she have what it takes? Maybe it's time to find out. She walks inside.

A well-dressed woman greets her at the door. She introduces herself as Mrs. Hunt and asks

Joanna a few questions. Then she asks Joanna to "model" the clothes she is wearing. Joanna feels shy but does her best. She is relieved when Mrs. Hunt tells her that she could definitely be a top model.

Mrs. Hunt explains that Joanna needs to know a little more about make-up and hair styling. She will also have to learn how models walk and pose. However, in a short time she should be making top dollars as a model.

Joanna is thrilled. She tries to concentrate while Mrs. Hunt explains about the modeling school, but her mind is on high fashion. It seems that Joanna will have to attend the school for six months before the agency will try to place her. This will cost $100 a month. Joanna thinks that sounds like a fair price. After all, soon she will be making nearly $100 for one hour's work as a top model.

Mrs. Hunt gives Joanna a set of contract papers to sign. She explains that it is the agreement to attend school and pay the monthly fee.

As Joanna is about to sign, Mrs. Hunt asks, "You are 18, aren't you?"

Joanna pauses for an instant. It is clear that she must be 18 in order to qualify.

"Oh yes," she lies, "I was 18 on

my last birthday." Quickly Joanna signs the papers. Now she is on the way to a bright new career.

After a week of lessons, Joanna begins to wonder. She seems to know more about make-up and hair styling than the young woman teaching her. She checks with some of the other students. She finds that Mrs. Hunt has given them all the same encouragement. It is obvious to Joanna that some of them do not "have what it takes." She starts asking questions about which graduates the agency has placed. It turns out that the six-month course is no guarantee of work at all.

Joanna is depressed. The $100 a month fee is a drain on her small salary. She wishes she never signed the contract.

Your Turn

1. Why do you think Mrs. Hunt asked Joanna if she was 18? What difference do you think Joanna's age could make to the contract?

2. Do you think Joanna should keep to the terms of the contract? Why or why not?

When contracts can be canceled . . .

Legally, a person does not become an adult until reaching

an age set by law. This age varies from state to state but is usually from 18 to 21 years. Anyone under that age is known as a *minor*. In the story above, for example, Joanna was a minor. In her state, the age of adulthood (also known as *majority*) was 18.

Usually, it is not against the law for minors to make contracts. But in many cases minors do not have to live up to the terms of a contract they make. They have the right to cancel it if they want.

Why can minors get out of contracts? Under the law, all parties to a contract must be persons who can give "sane and intelligent consent."

Now, minors may be sane and intelligent in everyday terms, but most of them lack experience in dealing with contract situations. So the law says that minors do not have the maturity of judgment to give "sane and intelligent consent."

For example, if Joanna had been more experienced, she would have been aware of some of the sales techniques used by Mrs. Hunt. She might have waited to sign the contract until she checked out the school and agency.

Can Joanna get out of her contract? Yes. She can cancel the contract for any reason—or for no reason at all. She can cancel it even though she lied to Mrs. Hunt about her age. However, if she decides to get out of the contract, she must do it within a reasonable time.

. . . And when contracts cannot be canceled

In most states, minors are not allowed to cancel contracts for "necessities." These usually include food, clothing, shelter, medical care, and educational expenses.

What about an adult who makes a contract with a minor? The adult is *not* allowed to cancel the contract. It makes no difference whether the contract is for "necessities" or not. It also makes no difference whether the adult knows or does not know that the other party is a minor. In other words, Mrs. Hunt cannot break the contract with Joanna even though Joanna lied about her age.

Your Turn

1. Why do you think minors are usually held responsible for contracts for necessities?

2. Teenagers may cancel a contract "within a reasonable time." What do you think this means? Would it be the same time

for all contracts? What do you think would be a reasonable time in Joanna's case?

Action Project

1. Write a report on how your state deals with minors and contracts. You can get this information at your school or public library. Or you can call a lawyer who has visited your class or contact your State Bar Association. You should find out:
• the age of majority;
• if it is legal for minors to make contracts;
• what contracts minors may cancel;
• if there are special rules for contracts for necessities. If so, what items are considered "necessities" in your state?

2. Hold a class debate on this topic:

RESOLVED: Minors over the age of 14 should have same legal obligations as adults in carrying out contracts.

First, have each student make up two lists of arguments—those in favor of the resolution and those against it.

Next, the class should divide into two teams (by drawing lots). Each team should discuss the issue for 10 to 15 minutes and choose two of its members to present their arguments.

After the debate, write a paper saying what rights and responsibilities you think minors should have in making contracts.

2. Contracts that don't hold good

A contract that holds good under the law is known as a *valid* contract. We have just seen one type of contract that does *not* have to hold good. This is a contract made by a minor. Unless it is for necessities, the minor can cancel the contract and make it *invalid*.

There are two main types of contracts that do not hold good under the law. First there is the *void* contract. This is a contract that was invalid right from the start. For example:
• A valid contract must include an offer, an acceptance, and (in most states) consideration. A "contract" that does not include these three elements is void. Under the law, it never existed.
• A valid contract must be made for a legal purpose. If two criminals make an agreement to rob or kill, their contract is void. In the same way, if two businessmen make an agreement

to "fix prices" or form a monopoly, there is no valid contract.

Second, there is the *voidable* contract. A contract made by a minor is one example. This means that the minor can cancel the contract if he or she wants. But the minor also can let the contract hold good.

A contract is voidable if:
• It is made by people who are legally not "sane and intelligent." In addition to minors, these include people who are insane, mentally ill, or mentally weakened by sickness or old age.
• One of the parties made the contract unwillingly. For example, the other party may have used fraud, undue pressure, or the threat of violence.

A valid contract? You decide

Here are two case studies involving different kinds of contracts. As you read them, look for clues to tell you whether the contracts are valid, void, or voidable. For example:
• Does the contract include the elements of offer, acceptance, and consideration?
• Are all of the parties involved capable of sane, intelligent, and willing consent?
• Is the contract made for legal purposes?

Learning to fly

Mr. Janssen is nearly 80 years old. Almost every day his youngest daughter Alma comes to his home to help with the cleaning and to buy groceries. Sometimes Mr. Janssen is very alert and discusses the news with Alma. He also talks about the past. As a young man, he was one of the first airline pilots. Other times, Mr. Janssen seems confused. He cries a lot and won't talk. Alma thinks he ought to go to a nursing home and receive full-time care. But he gets angry when she mentions this idea.

One morning, Mr. Janssen awakes feeling excited. He is going to fly again. He finds an ad for a flying school in the newspaper and makes an appointment for an interview that morning. He phones for a taxi and arrives at the school before noon.

The flying instructor and Mr. Janssen talk about the old days. The instructor explains some of the changes that have taken place in aircraft since that time. Mr. Janssen is eager to learn to fly the new planes. He insists upon signing a contract for a series of lessons costing $500.

Next day, Alma arrives to help her father. She sees a copy of the contract lying on the hallway table. "What's this?" she asks.

"How should I know?" Mr. Janssen answers. "Maybe it's yours."

Your Turn

1. Is this a valid contract? Why or why not?

2. Suppose Mr. Janssen were 30 years younger and in good health. What kind of contract would this be then?

A promise is a promise

Jonathan Smoot is a kindly fellow. He always tries to treat people fairly and honestly. He has a great deal of money and sometimes people take advantage of him. But, on the whole, people treat him as well as he treats them.

Mr. Smoot is especially fond of Henry, the gardener. One day he has a long talk with Henry. He says how much he appreciates the fine work that Henry has done over the years. And in return for that work, Mr. Smoot will give Henry the guest cottage and an acre of land. Henry is delighted.

Time passes. Mr. Smoot seems to forget about his promise. Occasionally Henry mentions it and Mr. Smoot mutters, "Oh, yes, yes, I really must take care of that."

offer his estate for sale. When Henry hears about this, he is furious. He jumps into his car and drives over to Mr. Smoot's estate. Mr. Smoot is in the study.

"You made me a promise," Henry snarls. "And I'm going to make you keep that promise. You sign that guest house over to me right now or I'm going to tear you and the whole place apart."

Mr. Smoot begins to shake. He is frightened. "All right, Henry, all right. Whatever you say."

Mr. Smoot signs the contract. Henry leaves content. At last, the guest house is his.

Your Turn

1. Is this a valid contract? Why or why not?

2. Suppose Mr. Smoot had signed an agreement to give Henry the guest house *before* Henry lost his temper. Would that be a valid contract? Why or why not?

Action Project

Make up a case study involving a valid, voidable, or void contract. Exchange case studies with another student in the class. Look through the case study you have received and decide whether it is valid, voidable, or void.

Then Mr. Smoot has some money problems. He is forced to drop the members of his household staff. Henry is the last to be dismissed.

"Will I still get the guest house?" Henry wants to know.

"Certainly," Mr. Smoot replies, "in time, in time."

But the money problems get worse. Finally Mr. Smoot has to

3.
A special problem: at-home sales contracts

With contracts to buy something, it's usually the consumer who makes the first move. It's the consumer who walks into the store, or makes a phone inquiry, or answers a "for sale" ad. Of course, sometimes consumers may be talked into buying things they don't really want. But usually they have had a chance to think about what they want beforehand.

Door-to-door sales are different. Here it's the salesman who makes the first move. The customer has not had a chance to think about the purchase beforehand. And door-to-door salesmen have a big advantage, because people are used to treating visitors in their home as guests. So it's not surprising that quite a lot of customers have second thoughts about at-home sales contracts.

In some areas, laws have been passed curbing door-to-door sales. But companies can find ways around these restrictions. This story about an at-home sales contract is one example.

A free gift

Mrs. Vasquez is tired. It was a hard day at work. She opens her front door and checks the mail slot. Quickly she leafs through the letters. Bills, bills, and more bills. Then something catches her eye. It's a letter that says:

"Congratulations! You are one of a special group of qualified customers to whom this offer is being made. To receive your free gift—a complete gardening guide—just call 646-8976. A representative of 'Green Growth' will arrange to deliver your guide to your home. No obligations!"

"Why not?" Mrs. Vasquez thinks. She calls the number and arranges to have the gardening guide dropped off the following day, a Saturday.

About 10:00 a.m. on Saturday, the doorbell rings. It is Mr. Jonas, the representative from Green Growth. He congratulates Mrs. Vasquez and says there are just a few questions he would like to ask her.

Soon he is inside the house. He explains that he doesn't usually work Saturdays but that he wanted Mrs. Vasquez to have her guide as soon as possible.

Mr. Jonas talks and talks. He explains some of the new programs Green Growth offers. He says that Green Growth can take care of all her gardening

needs for only pennies a day.

By 11:50 Mrs. Vasquez is getting tired. Mr. Jonas is still explaining the service and she wishes he would leave. Still, he has given her so much of his time. And he did make a special trip to her house to bring her the gift on Saturday. So she agrees to sign the contract.

The next day Mrs. Vasquez thinks maybe she shouldn't have signed. She doesn't really need the service. The day after that, Mrs. Vasquez is sure she shouldn't have signed. Re-reading the contract, she discovers that the charge isn't just "a few cents a day" but almost $20 a week.

Your Turn

1. Do you think Mrs. Vasquez gave willing consent to the Green Growth contract?

2. Do you think she should be able to cancel the contract if she wishes? Why?

Canceling the contract

In recent years, some states have passed laws to protect consumers who sign at-home sales contracts. These laws allow buyers to cancel a home sales contract under certain conditions. For example, in California and New York, the buyer is given three days in which

to cancel any contract for goods or services costing over $50.

Suppose Mrs. Vasquez lives in California. After two days, she has decided she doesn't like the contract with Green Growth. She can now cancel it simply by writing a letter telling the company of her wish to cancel. The mailed notice becomes effective as soon as it is dropped into the mailbox.

Action Project

Call a local consumer protection agency in your area. Find out about the laws regarding home sales in your state. Then write out answers to the following questions:

• In your state, can an at-home sales contract be canceled? If so, under what conditions? For example:

• Is there a time limit? Must the contract hold good if the customer does not cancel it within that time limit?

• Must certain conditions be met? For example, must the customer give a reason for canceling the contract?

• Must the customer cancel the contract in a special way? For example, must he or she notify the company by registered mail?

4.
Broken contracts

A contract is broken when one of the parties fails to keep any promise made under the contract. This promise may be the whole of the contract or just a small part of it. Either way, the contract is considered broken. This is known as *breach of contract.*

In some cases, it can be legal to break a contract. This happens when the party breaking the contract has a *legal excuse*—that is, a reason good enough to be accepted by the law. For example:

• Mr. Davis promises to buy Mr. Smith's car for $3,000 on one condition. Mr. Smith must provide Mr. Davis with a mechanic's report stating that the car is in excellent shape.

The mechanic's report states that the car is in good condition but not excellent shape. Mr. Davis refuses to buy the car. He does not have to carry out his promise because Mr. Davis has not met the conditions of the contract. *Failure to meet conditions is a legal excuse.*

• Dave agrees to take care of Karen's house while she goes on vacation. She promises to pay him $50 a month plus food. Before vacation time arrives, Karen decides she would rather stay at home. Dave also has had second thoughts. He has enough worries trying to take care of his own house. They both agree to drop their contract. Neither of them can be charged with a breach. *Agreement to drop the contract is a legal excuse.*

Taking it to court

Suppose one of the parties breaks the contract *without* a legal excuse. What happens then? What can the other party do about it?

If the breach is slight, the other party may be wise to ignore it. Suppose Joan arranges to buy a necklace from Mary for $25. Joan promises to pay on Thursday evening, but does not hand the money over until Friday morning. Unless the delay causes big problems for Mary, she has nothing to gain by taking further action.

However, the breach may be serious. Suppose Mary needed the money for some urgent purpose, and Friday was too late. In a case like that, the injured party could go to court.

What happens when a breach of contract is taken to court? First, the court will decide whether the contract has in fact been broken without legal excuse. If so, it will then determine what the injured party has lost as a result. And it will order the party to make good this loss.

The injured party can ask for the loss to be made good in two different ways. These are: (1) by paying money, and (2) by carrying out the contract.

Money payment to cover the loss is known as *recovery of damages*. The injured party has suffered "damage" which can be made good by money. The amount of money to be paid will depend on the amount of damage. For example:

Mrs. Diaz owns a bookstore. She has a customer who wants to buy two sets of encyclopedias at $400 each. She orders these from the publisher and pays $300 for each set. If the company fails to deliver the sets, Mrs. Diaz can sue for damages. She can ask for, and probably win, $800. This covers not only the $600 she paid but also the $200 profit she would have made on the two sets.

In some cases, money cannot make up the injury to the suing party. The court may then order the other party to carry out the terms of the contract exactly. For example:

Maria has been saving her

84

money for some time. She wants to buy a beautiful belt from a Navajo jewelry store down the street. She goes into the shop and makes an offer to the owner. He accepts. Maria pays for the belt and asks him to clean it for her while she does some shopping.

When she comes back, the owner tells her that he has changed his mind. The belt is worth far more than he charged. He says he now doesn't want to sell it at all at any price.

If Maria sues the store owner, she may ask for the contract to be carried out. She may feel that no other belt can match the one she wanted, and money cannot make up for the injury. If the court agrees, it may order the store owner to give Maria the belt she chose. This kind of award is often made in law suits dealing with something that is unique, such as a specific piece of land or a rare object.

Field Activity

Arrange to visit a court where a breach of contract case is to be heard. Keep a record of the case by using these headings: type of court; date of visit; presiding judge; plaintiff (suing party); defendant (party being sued); brief description of the case; procedures followed; court decision; award (if any). Under the "procedures" heading, make sure to note the roles played by each person involved in the case.

Following the court visit, role-play a mock trial. If possible, invite an attorney specializing in contracts or a judge to visit your class. Ask him or her to help prepare arguments, set up the role-play and possibly take the part of the judge. Here are suggested steps in preparing and conducting the trial:

1. As a class activity, make up a case in which a contract is broken without lawful reason.

2. Select members of the class to play the roles of the parties to the contract and their attorneys.

3. Select class members to play the roles of the various court officials.

4. Plaintiffs and their attorneys should prepare arguments to support their position. They should also decide whether to ask for damages or the carrying out of the contract.

5. Defendants and their attorneys should prepare arguments to support their position.

6. Students role-play the case.

7. The judge decides the case.

Contracts:
a Bibliography

Teenagers and the Law
by John Paul Hanna, Ginn, 1975.
Covers many areas of the law,
including business rights, torts,
(Part 4), and family law (Part 5).

The Law and You
by Elinor Porter Swiger,
Bobbs-Merrill, 1973.
Presents everyday situations
involving many aspects of the
law, including contracts.

You and the Law
Reader's Digest, 1973.
A reference book on all aspects of
the law.

PART 3
HOUSING LAW

Chapter 7

Renting a Home

Ann was tired and so was Lynn. It had seemed like such a good idea — commuting the 30 miles between their homes and college. But they hadn't counted on the rush hour traffic. Sometimes, like today, it took nearly two hours to go one way.

"Just think what it's going to be like at final exam time," said Ann. "We'll spend more hours driving than studying. I really think we ought to get an apartment close to the school."

Lynn nodded. "We'd probably have to get part-time jobs to help pay our expenses. But I'd rather be working than sitting in a car any day."

"Me too," Ann answered. "I think I'll talk to my folks about it tonight."

"I wonder how we'd find a place?" Lynn asked. "And how much we'd have to pay?"

The decision to find a place to live away from home is one that most of you probably will make within the next few years. And chances are you will have some questions just as Lynn and Ann do.

How do you find a place to live? How much should you pay? What *papers do you have to sign? What are your legal rights? Do you have responsibilities?*

In this unit we will try to find answers to these and other important questions. Most young people, like Ann and Lynn, will start out renting a place to live. So this chapter deals with rentals. Chapter Eight covers the legal questions involved in buying a home.

1. Landlords and tenants

The area of law that covers rentals is called landlord-tenant law. Some of its ideas go all the way back to the days of feudal England. In those days only the king owned land. However, he allowed various lords to "hold" parts of it. The lords could then "rent" their holdings to other people in return for food, money, or services. That's how we get the word landlord.

In feudal England the landlord had very few responsibilities toward tenants—the people who rented the land. As a result, most landlord-tenant disputes were decided in favor of the landlord. These decisions formed part of what is known as *common law*. In other words, they were based not on written regulations but upon custom and common sense.

Many English landlord-tenant laws were brought to this country with the colonists and remain in some form today. In common law, the landlord is still usually favored over the tenant. In recent years, however, many states have decided that old landlord-tenant laws are unfair. These states have passed laws that divide rights and responsibilities more evenly between landlords and tenants.

Since most landlord-tenant laws are created at the state and local level, they can differ widely from place to place. However, many of these laws are based on principles that are the same in most or all states. We will take a look at some of these on the following pages.

Finding a place to rent

That night Lynn and Ann each spoke with their parents about renting an apartment. The parents agreed that the girls needed to live closer to the college. Next day, Ann and Lynn started to look for an apartment.

First they checked the bulletin board outside the student union. Two rentals were advertised, but both had been taken already.

They decided to take a drive

around the streets nearby. They found a couple of "for rent" signs but both buildings looked old and run down.

"Well, I guess that leaves the newspaper," Lynn said cheerily.

Lynn and Ann drove to a coffee shop, bought a newspaper and looked through the classified section.

"There are so many!" Lynn moaned. "How on earth are we going to pick one? How do we even know which ones to call? Some don't even have addresses."

"Here, how about this one?" Ann asked. "At least it's cheap. We can call and find out more about it."

Lynn made the call and whispered the information to Ann. "She says it's a single, whatever that is, and it's $75 a month."

"Ask her if it would be big enough for two people," Ann said.

"She says of course it wouldn't be big enough for two people. A single is only one room and a bathroom. Oh, and it's way over on the other side of town," Lynn whispered.

Ann shook her head. Lynn thanked the woman and hung up.

"That was kind of scary," she said with a laugh. "The woman wanted to know all about me. How old I am. What I do. Whether

I have a job. I felt like I was asking her for a favor. Well, at least we know what a single is."

After a few more phone calls, the girls found out about a lot of other kinds of apartments too. They found out that a studio is one very large room with kitchen and bathroom. Apartments advertised as "one bedroom" or "two bedroom" also have a living room as well as kitchen and bathroom.

Of course, the rooms could vary widely in size.

The last number they called turned out to be a real estate agency specializing in rentals. By this time, the girls had decided they could use some help. They agreed to come in on Saturday to speak with the real estate agent.

Action Project

Look at the classified section of your local newspaper. Try to figure out the real estate "shorthand" used in various ads. Then ask yourself these questions:

1. Do the rentals in some areas appear to be more desirable than in other areas? More expensive? More plentiful? Why?

2. If you were looking for an apartment, which ones do you think you would call about? Why?

Meeting the landlord

The real estate office obviously did a lot of business with students from Byron. The school colors were on the walls, along with pictures of the football and basketball teams. The girls felt right at home.

"All right, let's be logical about this," said Mr. Singleton, the real estate agent. "First of all, where would you like to live?" He

showed them a large map of the city of Byron.

Lynn and Ann pointed to the area they were interested in.

"All right," Mr. Singleton said. He began to flip through a large book of rental listings. "Here's a two-bedroom that rents for $350 a month. It looks like a nice place."

The girls looked at each other with disappointment. "That's far too much money," Lynn said. "Isn't there anything cheaper?"

"Well, let's see," Mr. Singleton said. "Now here's a studio apartment that's big enough for two people. It's right next to the landlord's home and it rents for $175 a month."

"That's perfect," Lynn said happily.

Ann nodded in agreement.

"Uh-oh," Mr. Singleton added. "It says here, 'No students.' "

"Why not?" Lynn asked.

"Only one way to find out." Mr. Singleton picked up the phone. As he spoke with the landlord, Ann wondered if it was legal for the landlord to bar students. Then Mr. Singleton hung up.

"Well?" Lynn asked.

"He's very leery," Mr. Singleton said. "Seems the last time he rented to students, they practically wrecked the place. There were loud parties—trash piled

up—broken furniture. This guy isn't too crazy about your kind of people. Still, he did agree to interview you. And if you seem all right to him, you can have the place."

Lynn and Ann were nervous as they walked up the steps to Mr. Lee's house. "This is worse than going for a job," Ann whispered to Lynn.

They had dressed very carefully and both looked neat and clean. They had even washed the car for the occasion.

The interview was brief. Mr. Lee saw that the two girls weren't like the students he had rented to last time. He explained what he expected from his tenants and what they could expect from him as landlord.

Your Turn

1. Suppose you were a landlord who wished to rent an apartment next to your house. What kinds of things would you want to know about tenants wishing to rent the apartment? Are there personal qualities you would look for? What questions would you ask?

2. Suppose you were a tenant. What kinds of things would you want to know about the landlord? The property? The terms of the rental?

2.
Choice of tenants

Mr. Lee may seem like a very picky landlord. But from his point of view, choosing the right tenants is very important. Many landlords prefer certain types of tenants over others.

For example, a landlord may not like to rent to people with children because of extra noise as well as wear and tear on the apartment. A landlord may prefer married tenants to unmarried ones in the belief that married people are more responsible. A landlord may not want to rent to someone who is unemployed. A landlord may not want to rent to people for many other reasons—some good, some bad.

Legally, just how picky can a landlord be? Here are two examples of a landlord who refuses to rent to a would-be tenant. One example is legal in most communities. The other is illegal everywhere in the United States.

Story No. 1

Jamie Wilson is a very successful black artist. He is looking for an apartment closer to his studio and sees an ad for one on the same street. He makes an appointment to see it. On the day of the appointment he doesn't have time to get cleaned up. So he arrives in his work clothes—old blue jeans and a shirt covered with splashes of paint. He's also wearing a necklace of blue beads.

The landlord opens the door, takes one look at Jamie and says, "I won't rent to you."

"You mean because I'm black?" Jamie asks.

"I don't care if you're green," the landlord answers. "I don't rent to hippie weirdos."

"I'm not a hippie," Jamie argues.

"Yeah?" the landlord says. "Well, you look like one and that's enough for me."

Story No. 2

Jerry Silverman needs to find a new place to live. He drives around the neighborhood he's interested in. He sees a large apartment building that looks perfect. He takes down the number to call that is written on the "for rent" sign in front of the building. When he gets home, he calls the landlord.

"Hello, Mr. Pritchard," Jerry says, "I'm calling about the apartment you have for rent."

Mr. Pritchard describes the apartment and the terms of the

rental. Jerry is interested and makes an appointment to see the place.

"Oh, by the way," Mr. Pritchard says, "what's your name?"

"Jerry Silverman," Jerry answers.

"Oh, that puts a very different light on things," Mr. Pritchard says. "I'm very sorry, Mr. Silverman, but we don't rent to Jews in this building."

Your Turn

Which of the stories do you think is an example of a legal reason for turning down a would-be tenant? Which do you think is illegal? Why?

Fair housing

In most communities, the landlord who turned down Jamie Wilson would be within his rights. As a private landlord, he is entitled to choose tenants on the basis of his likes and dislikes. He can turn down a would-be tenant because he doesn't like the way the person wears his hair or dresses or speaks. In fact, he can turn down a tenant for almost any reason at all.

There are some important exceptions. A landlord may not refuse to rent to someone because of that person's race, religion, sex, or national origin. The Federal Fair Housing Law of 1968, as amended in 1974, makes this illegal for all rental units with four or more apartments.

The landlord in the second example has broken the law. If Jerry decides to take action, he has three choices:

• He can bring a court action against Mr. Pritchard to end the discrimination. He may also ask for damages of up to $1,000.

• He can file a complaint with the Department of Housing and Urban Development. The Department will contact Mr. Pritchard and try to persuade him to obey the law. If other complaints have been made about the same landlord, the Department may take action in court.

• He can file a complaint with the Attorney General of the United States. Again, if there is other evidence of discrimination by the landlord, the Attorney General may try to end it with a court order.

Action Project

Most states and many communities as well have their own laws on discrimination in addition to the federal law. For example, some communities do not allow discrimination against unmarried tenants or families with children. Find out what kinds of laws, if any, your state and community have against discrimination. The class can then suggest and discuss any additions or amendments they would like to see in these laws. This discussion can serve as a springboard to the following simulation.

Simulation: landlord and tenant

What do you think are valid reasons for turning down a would-be tenant? What reasons do you think are not valid? As a class, write up your own "discrimination laws."

1. Divide the class into landlords and tenants. One-fourth of the students should be landlords who own apartment buildings. The remaining three-fourths should be tenants.

2. Students playing the parts of landlords should write an ad for any one of the apartments they own. They should place these ads on a bulletin board at the front of the class.

3. Students playing the parts of tenants should write short "biographies" describing: who they are; whether single or married; how many children, if

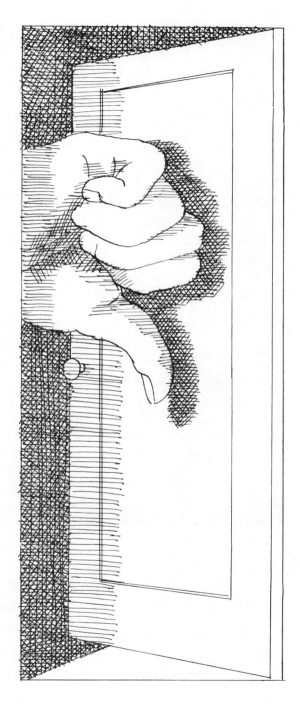

any; what work they do; leisure activities (for example, whether they like reading or whether they practice on the drums); and what kind of rental they are looking for.

4. "Tenants" check the bulletin board for rentals they think might fill their needs. Then they meet with the landlords renting those properties.

5. Tenants decide where they would like to live and landlords tell them whether they are accepted.

Following the simulation, discuss what took place in terms of these questions:

1. For what reasons were "tenants" accepted or turned down?

2. For those turned down, were the reasons fair or unfair according to the classroom "laws"? According to the Federal Fair Housing Law?

3.
What is a lease?

Luck was with Ann and Lynn. Mr. Lee liked them and decided to rent them the apartment for the six remaining months of their school year. He called Mr. Singleton and asked him to draw up the agreement papers.

As Ann and Lynn drove back to Mr. Singleton's office, they wondered what kind of papers Mr. Lee was talking about.

"Oh, it's all standard. Nothing unusual," Mr. Singleton explained when they were all back together again. "He just meant the lease agreement, and—"

"A lease?" Lynn broke in.

"Yes," Ann added. "What's a lease?"

Mr. Singleton smiled and leaned back in his chair. This is what he told the two girls:

A lease is a contract between the landlord and the tenant. It states the length of time that the property is to be rented, the rent that must be paid, and the responsibilities of the landlord and tenant.

For Lynn and Ann, the rental time would be six months. In this case, a spoken lease would be legal, since a contract has to be in writing only if it lasts for more than a year. However, a written lease can be used for any rental.

Ann looked at Lynn. "What do you think?"

"I don't know," said Lynn. "Suppose we don't like the apartment and want to move? If we sign a lease we're stuck there for six months."

"That's right," said Ann. "Is signing a lease the only way we

can rent the apartment?"

Mr. Singleton explained that sometimes a rental is made without any specific time limit. The contract is then called a rental agreement, not a lease. If Lynn and Ann made a rental agreement with Mr. Lee, they would be renting on what is called a "month-to-month" basis. This means that either the girls or Mr. Lee could end the agreement with only 30 days' notice. For example, suppose Lynn and Ann decided after three months that they wanted to move back home. They could then give notice to Mr. Lee and move out 30 days later, with no more obligation. Or suppose Mr. Lee decided he wanted to rent the apartment to someone else. He could give the girls 30 days' notice and they would have to leave.

"Oh," said Ann. "You mean we might want to stay, but Mr. Lee could tell us to leave? And he could do that even if he had nothing to complain about?"

Mr. Singleton nodded his head. "Yes, he could. But with a lease, you don't have that worry. As long as you meet your responsibilities, you're secure for the six months. Right now, Mr. Lee is offering you a lease. But in a month or two, he might change his mind again about renting to students."

Your Turn

1. A lease is a kind of contract. In Unit Two, you learned that a contract must include an offer, acceptance, and consideration. With Mr. Lee's rental, what is being offered? What is the consideration?

2. What advantages does a lease have over a rental agreement? What advantages does a rental agreement have over a lease? Which do you think Lynn and Ann should choose? Why?

Terms of the rental

"Suppose we do sign a lease," Lynn said to Mr. Singleton. "You mentioned some other papers, too. What else would we have to sign?"

"Oh, the only other thing is the security deposit," said Mr. Singleton. "It's something that most landlords ask for. You give the landlord a sum of money to hold for the period of the lease. This deposit can be used to pay for any repairs if you damage the apartment. Of course, that doesn't include normal wear and tear."

"What is normal wear and tear?" Ann asked.

"Well," Mr. Singleton said,

"after living in the apartment for a time you might wear down the carpeting near the front door. That would be normal wear and tear. It would be caused just by walking through the door. On the other hand, if you spilled a bottle of ink on the carpet and the landlord had to replace it, that *wouldn't* be normal wear and tear."

"If we don't damage anything in the apartment and just give it normal wear and tear, will we get our security deposit back?"

"Oh yes," Mr. Singleton

answered. "The landlord will return any part of the security deposit not used. That can be written in the lease."

"And how much will the security deposit cost?" Lynn and Ann both asked.

"Mr. Lee wants a sum equal to a month's rent. That would be $175," Mr. Singleton answered.

"Wow," Ann gasped. "That means we have to come up with $350.00."

The two girls looked at each other with worried expressions.

You be the judge

Whenever possible, a lease agreement should include a clear explanation of the security deposit. It should state the reasons for which it may be used and the conditions under which it may be returned to the tenant at the end of the lease.

However, many agreements do not include these details. Even when they do, they may not cover all possible problems. Suppose you were the judge in a Small Claims Court. In which of the

PERRIS HIGH SCHOOL

cases below do you think payments should be made from the tenant's security deposit?

Use "normal wear and tear" as your guideline. In other words, if you think the damage was caused by normal wear and tear, payment should *not* be taken from the deposit.

1. The tenant's cat has clawed the drapes to shreds.

2. The TV channel selector is worn out and has to be replaced.

3. The flooring is gouged because the tenant shifted heavy furniture around.

4. There are dart holes in the living room door.

5. The kitchen walls and counter have been damaged by continual splattering of hot fat.

6. Heavy rain came in through an open window and ruined part of the parquet floor.

Reaching a decision

Lynn and Ann were still trying to make up their minds about renting the apartment.

"I don't know," said Lynn. "It's a lot of money for a month's rent plus security. And if we signed the lease we'd be tying ourselves to a lot of promises."

"Yes," said Ann. "Just what promises would we make if we signed a lease?"

Mr. Singleton pushed a piece of paper across his desk. "This is a standard lease form," he said. (See next page.) "You'll find basically the same terms in lease forms all over the country. Of course, if the landlord and tenant agree, terms can be cut out, or changed, or added. However, Mr. Lee wants to use the form as is."

The two girls leaned forward and read through the form.

"Well," said Lynn, "I feel we're getting in deep with all this legal stuff. I mean, renting an apartment seems like a big responsibility."

Mr. Singleton nodded. "That's true. But if you carry out your part of the agreement and Mr. Lee carries out his part, you shouldn't have any problems. Of course, the decision is up to you. Give me a call later this afternoon and let me know what you decide."

Your Turn

1. What kinds of things do you think Lynn and Ann should take into account in deciding whether to sign a lease with Mr. Lee?

2. If Lynn and Ann decide to sign the lease, what questions should they ask about its terms?

Standard Lease Form

(simplified)

THIS LEASE, made this   day of   19
BETWEEN   , herein called lessor
and   , herein called lessee.

WITNESSETH: That lessor, in consideration of the agreements herein contained, does hereby lease, to lessee all that property in the city of   , County of   , State of   , described as: for the term of   , commencing on the   day of   , 19   , and ending on the   day of   , 19   , at the total rent or sum of   Dollars, payable in advance on the   day of each and every calendar month of said term in equal   payments of   Dollars.

This lease is made by lessor and accepted by lessee on each of the following conditions and terms:

Lessee hereby agrees as follows:

FIRST: To pay lessor said rent as above provided, and in addition to pay, when due, all water, electric, gas and other lighting, heating and power rents and charges in connection with said premises during said term;

SECOND: Not to let or sublet the whole or any part of said premises, or make or allow any alteration to be made in or on said premises, or put the same to any different use, without, in each instance, first obtaining the written consent of lessor;

THIRD: Not to commit or permit any waste on said premises, or any acts to be done in violation of any law or ordinance, and not to use or permit the use of said premises for any illegal or immoral purpose;

FOURTH: If any rent shall be due and unpaid or if default shall be made in any of the agreements on the part of lessee contained in this lease, lessor may without any notice, re-enter and take possession of said premises and remove all persons therefrom;

FIFTH: At the expiration of the said term, the said lessee will quit the premises in as good order and condition as reasonable use and wear thereof will permit, damages by the elements excepted.

WITNESS our hands, the day and year first above written.

4.
Tenant and landlord responsibilities

When you sign a lease or rental agreement, certain obligations are created for both you and the landlord. Many of these are stated in the terms of the lease or agreement. But certain obligations exist whether they are stated or not.

As a tenant, one of your most important responsibilities is to pay the rent. In most cases, rent is due in advance. For example, suppose Ann and Lynn did decide to sign the lease. They would have to pay the first month's rent before they moved into the apartment, and the second month's rent would be due at the beginning of the second month.

Another responsibility you have as a tenant is to take care of the rental property. You must not carve your initials in the kitchen counters, let sinks overflow onto the floors, or otherwise damage the property. If you have permission to keep a pet, you must not let it scratch the curtains or walls or stain the rugs. The terms of some rentals even bar you from hanging pictures on walls because you would make nail holes or tape marks.

Usually the lease or rental agreement makes clear who is responsible for keeping the property clean and making repairs. Often the landlord agrees to be responsible for any major repairs, and also for looking after the areas used by all tenants, such as stairways and walkways. The tenant is often responsible for making minor repairs and for taking care of property directly under his or her control.

As a tenant, you must not use the rental property for any reason other than that for which it was rented. In other words, if the apartment is rented to you as a home, you may not turn it into a dance studio without the landlord's permission.

You also must not make any changes in rental property without the landlord's approval—even if the changes are improvements. For example, you may not modernize the kitchen by putting in new cabinets and a built-in dishwasher unless the landlord agrees. And if he does agree, such improvements become part of the property and you may not take them with you when you leave.

Since most leases are written by or for landlords, the terms usually stress the responsibilities of the tenant. However, the landlord also has certain responsibilities. Legally, the landlord must meet these whether they are stated in the agreement or not.

One important responsibility of the landlord is to provide "quiet enjoyment of the premises." This means that he or she must not interfere with the tenant's daily life in the rented property or allow other tenants to do so. For example, suppose a rock-and-roll group wants to practice all night long in the apartment above yours. The landlord may not give them permission if it interferes with your quiet enjoyment of your apartment.

In the past, providing "quiet enjoyment" was the landlord's major responsibility, and sometimes the only one. However, in recent years, many states have decided that the landlord has other responsibilities.

Many states have passed laws requiring that rental property be "fit for people to live in." These laws require certain standards of rental housing. What is "fit" is determined by state and local housing codes which may differ from one place to another. The landlord is responsible for making certain that property he rents meets the proper "fitness" requirements.

These requirements usually come under three main headings: facilities, maintenance, and floor space. The chart below explains what these mean and gives some typical requirements for each.

Most housing codes cover:	Typical requirements:
FACILITIES Electricity; heat; kitchen and bathroom fixtures	Every kitchen sink, lavatory basin, and bathtub or shower shall be in good working condition and connected to an approved water and sewer system.
MAINTENANCE Foundations; ceilings; walls; stairways; windows; doors	Every stairway and every porch shall be in safe condition and sound repair. Every interior wall and ceiling shall be free of holes and large cracks.
FLOOR SPACE Minimum per occupant	Each occupant shall have a minimum of 100 square feet of livable space.

Housing codes and tenants

Many housing codes also include tenant responsibilities for keeping housing "fit to live in." The following are examples from one such housing code:

Every occupant of a family unit must:

a) keep that part of the family unit which he occupies in a clean and safe condition;

b) keep all plumbing and other fixtures in a clean condition and take reasonable care in their proper use;

c) keep all exits clear at all times;

d) exterminate any insects, rodents, or pests on the premises;

e) dispose of all garbage only in the containers required and place it in the containers in a clean manner;

f) not place on the premises any material which causes a fire hazard or otherwise endangers the health or safety of any occupant of the building.

Your Turn

1. Do you think the tenant responsibilities described above are fair? What about landlord responsibilities?

2. Are there any tenant responsibilities you would add? Remove? Landlord responsibilities?

Field Activity

Arrange a visit to your local housing authority, and appoint a group of 4 or 5 students to make the visit. The group should discuss the procedures followed when the authority receives a housing complaint. If possible, they should also observe part of these procedures being carried out.

5. When the tenant breaks a lease

When landlords or tenants do not live up to their responsibilities, there is a breach of the rental or lease agreement. This is the same as a breach of contract, discussed in Unit Two. If the breach is not serious, the landlord and tenant may try to put it right.

For example, a landlord discovers that a tenant is keeping a pet in violation of the agreement. Rather than end the agreement, he or she usually just asks the tenant to get rid of the pet.

Or a tenant feels that the landlord is violating their agreement by not providing "quiet enjoyment." Here, too, he or she may simply ask the landlord to correct the situation rather than end the agreement.

Sometimes, though, a breach is so serious that it cannot be repaired. Then the lease or rental agreement is broken. If the tenant is the cause of the breach, there are certain actions the landlord may take. If the landlord is the cause of the breach, there are actions the tenant can take. We will first explore some of the ways the landlord can deal with a tenant breach.

A very common breach occurs when a tenant decides to leave before the lease has ended. There can be many reasons for this. Tenants may decide to move to another part of town or even to another city or state. They may decide that the rental does not fit their needs. Or they may simply discover that they cannot afford to pay the rent. The following is an example:

A new job
Mr. Jennings leases an apartment in his building to Mr. Baron for a period of one year. After six months, Baron is transferred to work in another city. He tells Jennings he will not be able to fulfill his lease.

At this point, Jennings has several choices. He can agree to release Baron from the contract and look for a tenant to take out a new lease. He can allow Baron to sublet the apartment—that is, to find someone else to rent it for the rest of the lease period. He himself can try to rent it to someone else for that period. Or he can allow the apartment to stay vacant until the lease period is over.

If Jennings releases Baron from the contract the lease is ended. Baron then has no further responsibility to Jennings. If Jennings allows Baron to sublet, Baron will still be responsible for any rent the new tenant fails to pay as well as for any damage done to the property. If Jennings tries to rent it to someone else, without ending the lease, he may be able to collect damages from Baron for any time the apartment stays vacant. If he allows the apartment to stay empty, he may be able to charge Baron for rent until the end of the lease period. In some states, however, a landlord cannot do this. He or she can charge the previous tenant only after trying and failing to re-rent.

Your Turn
What do you think are some

107

advantages and disadvantages of each of the choices available to Jennings? If you were Jennings, what do you think you would do?

Staying put

In the previous example, the tenant broke his lease agreement by leaving the apartment. However, with other types of breach of agreement, the tenant may want to stay. In these situations, the landlord may take legal steps to have the tenant *evicted* or removed from the property. The landlord might do this if the tenant fails to pay the rent, damages or misuses the property, or refuses to leave when a lease period is ended. The following is a case in point:

A tough tenant

Janet Browne rents an apartment to Morris Brand. Morris signs a one-year lease and agrees to pay $200 a month in rent. After three months, he misses a rent payment. When Janet goes to see him about this, she discovers that he is using the apartment to teach karate classes. As she stands at the door talking with him, she sees seven students vigorously practicing in the living room. She can see that some of the furniture has been damaged and that the wall-to-wall carpeting has been worn through in several places. She asks Morris to move out. He refuses.

In this case, Janet has three possible grounds for evicting the tenant. One, Morris has not paid his rent. Two, he has used the apartment for purposes other than those for which it was rented. And three, he has damaged the property.

Janet decides to begin eviction proceedings. Since nonpayment of rent is the easiest charge to prove, she decides to base her case on this.

Janet checks with her lawyer, who explains the eviction procedures in her state. The first step is to give Morris a written notice allowing him three days to move out and explaining that the reason is for nonpayment of rent. The lawyer explains that if Morris pays the rent he owes within that time, he will not have to leave. If he does not pay, she can proceed to evict him.

Janet writes the notice and hands it to Morris the next morning as he is carrying down his garbage. Then she waits for three days. She is hoping that he will *not* pay the back rent. He doesn't.

She then files a lawsuit at the

county courthouse. A copy of the complaint and a summons are handed to Morris as he is unloading groceries from his car. The papers explain that Morris has five days to respond to the complaint.

Morris does nothing. As a result, Janet wins the suit by default. Morris is ordered to leave the property. And Janet is awarded damages—the amount of rent due her. Morris pays what he owes and moves out with no further fuss.

If Morris had refused to leave, Janet could have gone to the sheriff for help. The sheriff would have delivered a notice to Morris stating that he must move within five days or be removed by force.

Your Turn

1. Do you think the eviction procedure described is fair to the landlord? The tenant? Do you think eviction is a reasonable step for a landlord to take for nonpayment of rent? Violating the lease? Staying on after a lease has expired?

2. Find out what the eviction procedures are in your state. How are they similar to the procedures followed by Janet's state? How are they different?

6.
When the landlord breaks a lease

Now we will take a look at the steps a tenant can take if the landlord is the cause of the breach. First of all, the tenant can decide whether he or she wants to end the tenancy or stay put and try to repair the breach. Here is an example of a couple who chose not to leave:

A new water heater

A young married couple, Roy and Jenny, move into their very first apartment in the state of Oklahoma. As a condition of the lease agreement, the landlord has agreed to replace an old and inefficient water heater within 30 days. Month after month Roy and Jenny wait for their new heater. They remind the landlord of their agreement several times, but he still does nothing. Finally, Roy and Jenny buy the water heater themselves and have it installed. They deduct the cost from their next rent payments.

A number of states give tenants the right to take this kind of action. If the landlord fails to make necessary repairs, the tenants can do so and deduct at least part of the cost from their rent payments.

The details vary from state to state. For example, in some states a tenant must get permission from the court before withholding rent. In many, there are limits on the amount of money that can be withheld. In California, for instance, tenants may not deduct more than one month's rent in a year. This means that tenants may not be able to recover all of the money they spend to make necessary repairs.

Your Turn

1. Do you think withholding rent is a fair way to solve the problem of landlords who fail to make necessary repairs? What advantages does it provide the landlord? The tenant?

2. Find out whether tenants are allowed to withhold rent in your state. If so, find out what procedures must be followed and whether there are conditions under which the tenant gives up the right to withhold rent for repairs.

Unfit to live in

Sometimes the problem goes beyond one or two repairs. What can a tenant do if the rental property is not fit to live in? If it doesn't meet local housing codes? Here is one example:

110

Brown v. Southall Realty Company

Mrs. Lillie Brown rented a basement apartment from the Southall Realty Company in Washington, D.C. The company had previously been warned of several housing code violations in the apartment. These included a toilet that didn't flush, a broken railing, and a ceiling lower than the legal minimum for living quarters.

The owner of the property had given the Housing Division a sworn statement that the basement would remain vacant until the violations were corrected.

Even though the representative of the realty company knew about the code violations, he told Mrs. Brown that the basement was livable.

Mrs. Brown moved out before the end of the lease period. The Southall Realty Company sued her for $230 in back rent.

Your Turn

Do you think Mrs. Brown should have looked more carefully at the apartment before moving in? If you were the judge, would this affect your decision in the case? As the judge, how would you decide the case?

A complaint of unfit conditions may bring housing inspector (below) to check conditions. If there are violations, the landlord will be forced to correct them.

Ask your teacher for the result of this case. It is listed on page 31 of the teaching guide.

Legal pressure

Mrs. Brown decided to leave her home when she found it unfit to live in. Some tenants, however, prefer to stay and try to have violations corrected. They may do this by reporting the violations to the local housing authority.

When a housing authority receives a complaint, it takes these steps:

1. A housing inspector goes to look at the property. If he finds violations, the landlord is sent a report requiring that they be corrected. There is a time limit for making corrections—often between 30 and 90 days.

2. Most communities have a housing board of appeals. If the landlord disagrees with the report, he or she can present arguments to the board. After hearing this appeal, the board will cancel, change, or confirm the report.

3. If the landlord fails to make any required corrections, authorities can usually charge him or her with a misdemeanor. If found guilty, the landlord will be fined or even jailed.

4. If the landlord still fails to

make the corrections, many housing codes allow for an "order to vacate." This means that all tenants have to move out of the building until the corrections are made. An "order to demolish" may be given if the property endangers the health and safety of the community. For example, it may be in such bad shape that it could collapse at any moment. Because these orders cause hardship to tenants as well as landlords, they are used only in extreme cases.

Sometimes tenants are aware of violations but do not report them. There are several reasons for this. For one thing, improvements on property often lead to higher rents, and the tenant may not wish to pay more—or be able to do so. Then, too, as bad as it may be, the property is home to the tenant. He or she may be afraid of losing it through an order to vacate or demolish. The tenant may also be afraid of losing it another way, as the following case shows:

Edwards v. Habib

Yvonne Edwards rented an apartment from Mr. Habib on a month-to-month agreement. She discovered when she moved in that there were several housing code violations. She reported them to the housing authorities. When the inspector checked the apartment he found more than 40 violations.

Habib was sent a notice of the violations and an order to correct them. He then gave Mrs. Edwards a 30-day notice to leave the apartment.

She was sure that Habib was evicting her to get even with her for reporting the code violations.

Habib pointed out that Mrs. Edwards was a month-to-month tenant with no lease. Therefore, he argued, he had the right to evict her for any reason or for no reason at all.

Ask your teacher for the result of this case. It appears on page 32 of the teaching guide.

Your Turn

Do you agree with Habib's argument that he may evict Mrs. Edwards for *any* reason? If you were the judge, how would you decide the case?

Resource Person. Invite a housing inspector to visit your classroom to discuss problems of substandard housing in your community, the steps being taken to correct them, and methods of enforcement.

Chapter 8

A Home of Your Own

Are you planning to buy your own home?

That question probably seems far-fetched. For one thing, even renting a home may seem a long way in the future, and some people never buy one at all. Then, too, buying a home seems terribly complicated. Doesn't it take many thousands of dollars? And don't you have to find your way through a maze of legal procedures?

Buying a home isn't as difficult as many people imagine. After all, in Part One you learned about credit, and that's what most people use to help with the expense of buying a home. In Unit Two you learned about contracts, and these are the main legal procedures involved. So you already know much of the basic information needed in home buying.

In addition, some of the laws applying to homeowners can also affect people who live in rentals or homes owned by someone else. So it is already useful for you to know what's involved in being a homeowner.

1.
A question of money

Once you have decided upon the home that you wish to buy, there are several steps you should take.

The first step is to settle on a price for the property. Suppose you have found a nice one-bedroom house for sale. The owner is asking $32,000. You decide to offer $28,000. The owner refuses but makes a counter-offer to sell for $31,000. You refuse but make a new offer to pay $29,000. Eventually you may settle on a price somewhere in between—say, $30,000.

This does not mean that you have to be able to hand over a check for $30,000. Since very few people are in a position to pay cash for their homes, most home buyers apply for a special kind of loan called a *mortgage* (pronounced MOR-gidge).

A mortgage is a legal agreement which makes the property itself the security for the loan. For example, suppose you take out a mortgage for $20,000 from a bank or savings and loan company. You will repay that money, plus interest, in monthly installments. This is like an ordinary bank loan, except that the payments will be spread over many years. However, if you default on your mortgage, the lending company can begin "foreclosure proceedings" to take possession of your property. When a loan is foreclosed, the lender can sell the property to recover the amount you owe.

Usually lending companies will not allow a mortgage on the total cost of the home. Some will lend more than others, but you nearly always have to pay for the home partly in cash. This down payment can range from 10 to 30 percent of the total cost. With a $30,000 home, therefore, you might have to count on paying between $3,000 and $9,000 in cash.

In shopping for a mortgage, buyers should pay close attention to interest rates. Because you will be paying off the loan for a long time—perhaps 20 or 30 years—the total amount you pay in interest may be quite large. In fact, it may be more than the loan itself. A difference of only ½ percent can mean a lot in the actual dollars paid back.

2.
Making a contract

After you and the seller have agreed on a price, the next important step is to sign a *contract of sale.* What does this involve?

The contract of sale must contain the names and signatures of the buyer and seller, a statement that both parties agree to complete the sale, a description of the property, the price, and the date the sale is to be completed.

In addition, several other items are often included. Their purpose is to protect both the buyer and the seller and help to prevent future disputes. Because these items can make the contract rather complicated, most people consult a lawyer at this point.

The items often added to a contract of sale include:

1. A list of any restrictions on the property. Local laws may forbid certain ways of using the property or certain kinds of alterations. Suppose, for example, that a couple is planning to buy a particular building in order to open a restaurant. The listed restrictions may reveal that the entire area is zoned only for homes and that businesses are not allowed.

Sometimes buyers ask for a special clause to be added to the contract. This clause states that the contract can be canceled if there are restrictions it does *not* include.

2. A list of any debts affecting the property. Suppose the owner has used the house as collateral for a loan. If the debt has not been fully paid off, the creditor may be able to collect from the new owner. In some instances, the terms of such a loan may prohibit the owner from selling the property until the debt is paid.

3. A list of items to be included in the sale of the house. As a general rule, things that are permanently attached to the property are considered a part of it. For example, a built-in dishwasher would be considered a part of the house, while a portable dishwasher might not be. Still problems can arise when these items are not specifically described in the sales contract.

4. A statement of how the property is insured while the sale is being completed. Suppose the property is destroyed by fire or flood before the sale is completed. Or the property is vandalized. Who is responsible? Who is entitled to insurance benefits, if there are any? Must you still buy the property even if the house has been destroyed?

5. A statement of the type of financing arrangements the buyer expects to make. This can protect the buyer in case he or she is unable to obtain a suitable mortgage.

Action Project

Choose another member of the class to work with. Decide which of you will be the buyer and which will be the seller. (If necessary, toss a coin.) Then write a simple version of a contract of sale including all of the required terms and any others you think are important.

3.
Title to the property

The legal ownership of property is known as "title." Like "landlord," this word goes back to the days of feudal England. Lords were given different titles—such as duke or earl—according to the amount of land they held.

When you buy a home or a piece of land, you receive a title deed. (A deed is a legal document.) Before this happens, however, there must be a *title search*. This is done for two reasons: (1) to make certain that the seller actually owns the property and has the right to sell it, and (2) to find out whether there are any restrictions on the property.

The title search usually takes place in the county recorder's office. Records are examined to discover the legal owner of the property and any details that might affect the sale. Are there any mortgages on the property? Has the owner sold any rights in the property to someone else? Are there any restrictions on the way the property may be used? Is the property involved in any court judgment—for example, must it be used to pay off a debt?

If all goes well, you and the buyer meet to close the sale. The buyer receives the money and you receive the title deed. The deed is then recorded in the county recorder's office.

The sale is complete and you are now a homeowner.

4.
The new homeowner

As an owner instead of a tenant, you are likely to think of your home as your castle. It's a place you are free to enjoy and use as you wish. And you are right—but only up to certain limits. Here's an example:

Janice and Dan couldn't wait to move into their new home. At last they would be free from prying landlords and from rules, rules, rules. In their own home, they could do as they liked. They had purposely bought a house with a very large backyard. They were both expert dirt bike riders, and they wanted a place where they could set up hurdles and difficult runs. They planned to do a lot of practicing in the privacy of their own backyard.

At last the big day arrived. They moved in, arranged the furniture, and started work on the backyard runs. A week later they began practicing. Three days later, as they were riding their dirt bikes, their neighbor came to the fence. He asked them to stop. He complained that the fumes from the bikes were smelling up his yard and that the noise was driving him and his family crazy.

Janice and Dan refused. They told the neighbor it was their property and they could do anything they wanted with it.

Your Turn

1. Does the neighbor have any legal say in what Janice and Dan do on their own property? Why?

2. What steps, if any, should be taken to resolve the dispute between Dan and Janice and their neighbor?

3. Have you ever been involved in any similar dispute with a neighbor? If so, how was it resolved?

Nuisances

Your right to the "quiet enjoyment" of your property does have limits. Generally speaking, it must fit in with the right of other people to the quiet enjoyment of *their* property. If you do something that causes great interference with a neighbor's right, he or she may be able to take legal action.

This kind of interference is known as a *nuisance*. Here is a nuisance case dating back more than 350 years:

William Aldred's case

In 1611 William Aldred owned a house in England. The house was built in such a way that the entry hall and living room faced his neighbor's orchard. The house was only two feet from the property line. His neighbor Thomas Benton built a large wooden building that actually touched the property line. He then used the building as a pigsty. The pigsty blocked the light and view from Aldred's living room and the smell of the pigs filled that side of the house. Aldred took Benton to court.

Your Turn

1. Do you think the pigsty on Benton's property interfered with Aldred's right to the quiet

enjoyment of his own property?

2. Suppose Benton had no other place he could put his pigsty. Do you think this should make any difference to the court's decision?

Ask your teacher for the result of this case. It is listed on page 32 of the teaching guide.

Balancing people's rights

Today there seems to be endless opportunities for nuisance cases.

People play radios, stereos, pianos, and electric guitars. They work at home with electric drills and buzz saws. They have all kinds of ways to produce noise, fumes, smoke, and dust. However, most people accept a certain amount of give and take. They can live with a mild or occasional nuisance from a neighbor because they probably create some interference themselves.

The key question in legal cases is this: *How much* does the nuisance interfere with quiet enjoyment? Courts will usually try to decide whether it is a serious interference or simply an irritation. If it is an irritation, the courts will probably decide against the person making the complaint.

Suppose you are learning to play the violin and your practicing every afternoon drives the person next door wild. A court would probably decide that the benefits to you of playing the violin outweigh the interference with your neighbor's quiet enjoyment.

However, suppose you practice at 3:00 a.m. with all the doors and windows open and accompanied by a recording of a full orchestra. Now a court would probably decide that you are creating a nuisance and order you to stop.

You be the judge

In nuisance suits, the person complaining may not only ask the court to order the nuisance stopped, but also ask for damages. Look at the examples below and imagine that you are the judge. In each case, decide whether a nuisance does or does not exist.

1. The Smith family buys a dog to guard their property. The dog does a fine job but it barks and howls all night long. The neighbors on both sides ask the Smiths to put the dog in the house at night. The Smiths say that he will not be able to guard the property if he is inside.

2. Many of the women in Janet Lane's neighborhood are working mothers. Janet works in her home. Because she is home in the afternoons, she offers to take care of some of her neighbors' children after school. Every day the children arrive at 2:00 and play—often noisily—in Janet's backyard. The elderly woman next door complains that their noise keeps her from taking her usual afternoon nap and that they create a nuisance.

3. Larry Lewis is a carpenter. He does a great deal of work at his home. Often he works in the driveway between his home and his neighbor's. The work can be noisy and the wood shavings and sawdust drift over to his neighbor's flower bed. The neighbor tells Larry the noise is so loud that he and his wife can hardly carry on a conversation in their kitchen. He also says the sawdust and shavings are damaging his prize orchids. He asks Larry to work somewhere else. Larry refuses.

Other problems

A property owner may be held responsible for accidents that happen on his or her property. Suppose a tile falls off the roof and hits someone on the head. Or the barbecue grill sets fire to a neighbor's tree. Or the lawn sprinkler floods a neighbor's cellar. In each case the homeowner may be taken to court.

However, you don't have to be a property owner to face this kind of responsibility. Suppose that you drive a car and smash into someone's fence. Or you're riding a bike and knock someone down. Or you clout a baseball through someone's window. In these cases, too, you have caused damage and can be held responsible. We will look at this kind of problem in the next unit.

Chartread: Apartment plan

1. An apartment building has three floors, each laid out the same as shown in the plan. The local housing code applies to all buildings with more than four rental units. Does this building have to meet the requirements of the code?

2. The man who lives in Apartment B often puts garbage outside his front door early in the morning. He carries it down to the garbage cans an hour or two later. Does the tenant in Apartment A have any legal complaint? If so, on what grounds?

3. The tenant in Apartment B has a piano in his living room, opposite the kitchen door. He plays it every evening between 9 and 10 p.m. The tenant in Apartment A, who goes to bed early, complains that the playing disturbs his sleep. Suppose the case were taken to court and you were the judge. What decision would you make, and why?

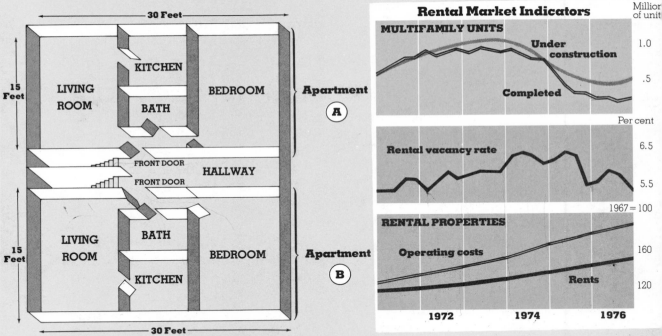

Federal Reserve Bulletin, March 1977

On the basis of the graph, mark each of these statements True, False, or Not Shown:

1. Fewer apartment buildings were constructed in 1976 than in 1974.

2. A larger percentage of apartments was occupied in 1972 than in 1974.

3. From 1972 to 1976, rents increased at a greater rate than the costs of running an apartment.

4. The total number of apartments available in 1976 was less than in 1973.

Housing Law:
a Bibliography

Landlord and Tenant
by George Ranney, Jr., and
Edmond Parker, Houghton Mifflin,
1974.
Covers rights and responsibilities
of landlords and tenants.

Your Legal Rights
As a Minor
by Robert H. Loeb, Jr., Franklin
Watts, 1974.
Covers many aspects of the law,
including housing, contracts (Part
2), and family law (Part 5).

Making the Law
Work for You
edited by Kenneth P. Norwick,
John Day, 1975.
Covers various aspects, including
housing and family law (Part 5).

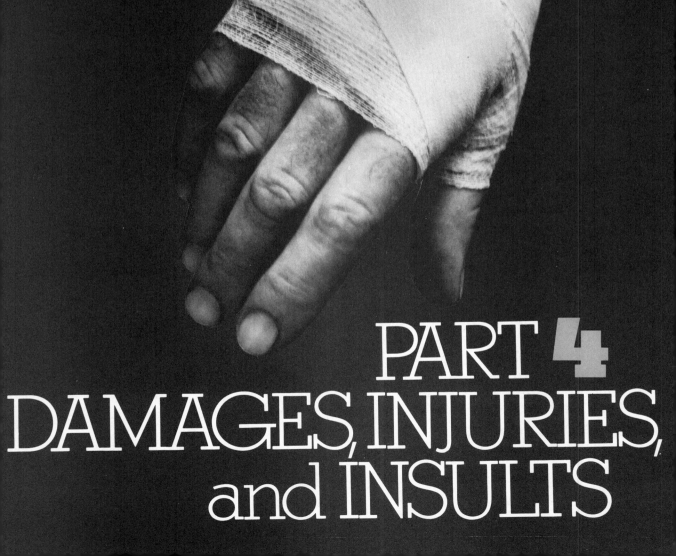

PART 4
DAMAGES, INJURIES, and INSULTS

Chapter 9

Mainly Accidental

Dan and Evelyn Turner were driving down the hill toward their home.

"There's Tommy up to his tricks," said Evelyn.

Ten-year-old Tommy Neece lived next door to the Turners. They often heard his temper tantrums when he didn't get his way. He also thought it was funny to put nails in the road. The Turners didn't like Tommy.

Right now he was riding down the sidewalk on his bicycle, pretending to be on a motorbike. As he reached the driveway of his house, he leaned to one side and made a skidding turn. The bike shot out into the street.

Dan's hands jerked hard on the steering wheel. The car swerved—not away from the bike but toward it. It hit the front wheel and threw Tommy to the ground, breaking his arm.

Howie Neece, Tommy's father, came running out of the house and knelt down by his yelling son. Then he shook his fist at the Turners.

"I'll sue you for this!" he shouted.

If Howie carries out his threat, he will file what is known as a *tort action*. The legal term "tort" comes from a French word meaning "wrong." It applies to cases where one person believes he or she has been wronged or harmed by another person. The plaintiff sues the defendant to recover *damages*—that is, a sum of money to make up for the harm done.

Different kinds of torts may involve different kinds of damages. In Howie's case, the damages would be for bodily injury. If the Turners' car had simply smashed the bike, the damages would be for property. In other cases, plaintiffs may ask payment for mental or emotional damage or even for damage to their reputation. If the harm was caused on purpose or by an extremely careless act, the plaintiff may also ask for *punitive* damages. This is money paid as a punishment.

Although there are many different kinds of torts, they can be divided into two main groups. Let's take another look at the case of Tommy's bicycle.

First, suppose the bike was smashed but Tommy was unhurt. And suppose Dan had been angry at Tommy and ran over the bicycle on a sudden impulse. That would be an *intentional tort*.

However, let's say it didn't happen that way at all. Instead, the driving seat suddenly shifted, causing Dan's hands to jerk the steering wheel. The damage to the bicycle was *unintentional*. It was what people call an accident.

Although torts come under civil law, they can sometimes lead to both civil and criminal actions. For example, suppose Dan Turner had had a fit of murderous rage and aimed his car at Tommy. Howie could still file a tort action to recover damages for Tommy's injury. But since attempted homicide is also a crime, the state could file criminal charges as well.

In this chapter we will explore the area of unintentional torts. Then, in Chapter Ten, we will look at the deliberate kind.

Field Activity

In the course of one day, look for any situations that might possibly involve or lead to a tort. For example: a collision or near-collision between two cars; an angry dispute between two people who might come to blows; children throwing rocks at one another; a truck with a dangerous projecting load, and so on.

Make a record of each situation under these headings: *Place; Time; Brief description of tort; What kind of injury? Accidental* or *intentional; Did the tort actually take place?*

Keep the record until you have finished studying this unit.

1. Accidents and carelessness

Many so-called accidents are really caused by someone's negligence or carelessness. In other words, they could have been avoided if the people involved had been more careful. When the carelessness of one party damages another, there may be grounds for a tort action.

Until the industrial revolution,

negligence suits were quite uncommon. But with the widespread use of machinery, the risks of negligence have increased tremendously. For example, since the automobile was invented, it alone has caused great damage to people and property through the carelessness of drivers, manufacturers, and dealers.

Suppose two people involved in an accident are *both* negligent. Can one sue the other for damages? In the past, the answer was usually no. Today, however, many states apply a rule known as *comparative negligence*. This means that courts try to decide each person's share of responsibility for the accident. If one person was more negligent, the other may be awarded some damages.

Today, negligence actions are so common that in many areas people involved in such suits must wait several years for a hearing. As a result, many negligence cases are settled out of court. That is, the plaintiff and defendant reach their own agreement on what damages, if any, are to be paid.

Damages awarded or agreed on in negligence suits may range from a few dollars to hundreds of thousands of dollars. Therefore, many people take out insurance to protect themselves against some kinds of negligence actions. For example, most drivers carry automobile insurance which includes liability coverage—that is, payment for damages to persons or property. In some states this type of auto insurance is required.

Proving negligence

What exactly is negligence? How can the plaintiff prove that the defendant was negligent?

To prove negligence, the plaintiff must be able to show all of the following:

1. The defendant took (or failed to take) an action.
2. The defendant had a duty to use care.
3. The defendant failed to use the proper care.
4. The plaintiff suffered damages.
5. What the defendant did (or failed to do) caused those damages.

Let's look at each of these in relation to the Turner/Neece case. Dan hit the bicycle unintentionally because the driver's seat shifted. Howie has filed suit against Dan for negligence. First Howie would have to show that Dan took or failed to take an action. That would probably not be difficult.

Dan admits that he was driving his car and swerved to the side.

Next, Howie would have to show that Dan had a duty to use care and failed to use the proper care. This might be a bit more difficult. So let's skip points two and three and come back to them later.

Howie would have to show that he suffered damages. If Tommy had pulled his bicycle out of the way of the Turners' car, there would be no injury and Howie could not sue Dan for negligence. To collect for negligence there must be actual damages. As another example, you could sue a negligent driver who drives over the curb and hits you. But you could not sue the same driver for negligence if you jumped out of the way and escaped injury at the last moment. However, in the story Tommy's broken arm is evidence of damage suffered.

Howie would now have to show that what Dan did (or failed to do) caused the damages suffered by his family. In this case, again, there is no problem here. Dan admits that in swerving to the side he ran into Tommy's bicycle.

Your Turn

Tommy would not have been injured if he had been riding his

bike properly. It shot out into the street because he was playing games. Do you think the court should take this into account? Is Tommy partly responsible for the "accident"? If so, does this clear Dan of all responsibility? Of some responsibility? Or should it make no difference?

The reasonable person

Now let's go back to points two and three—the duty to use care and failure to use the proper care. What is meant by "using care"? In the Neece/Turner case, should Dan have checked the seat catch every time he took the car out? Should he have prepared himself better for an emergency so that he wouldn't jerk the wheel? How does a court decide whether someone has a duty to be careful and whether that person was careful enough?

For some answers, here is an interview with Arnold Cohen, an attorney who specializes in negligent torts.

Interviewer: Every person is slightly different. You yourself would probably know whether you were being careful or not in a particular situation. But how do you judge whether someone other than yourself was careful in a negligence case?

Mr. Cohen: You're talking about feelings. But in a court of law, the defendant's feelings about whether he was careful enough are beside the point. Instead, we use a fairly objective standard.

Interviewer: How can you do that? It seems to me that the proper care would vary in different situations.

Mr. Cohen: Well, courts use what is sometimes called the standard of the "reasonable person." In other words, did the defendant do what a "reasonable person" would have done in the same situation? Naturally, this *would* vary from one situation to another.

Interviewer: But what is a reasonable person? That seems terribly vague.

Mr. Cohen: First of all, the reasonable person is usually considered to have average intelligence and average capabilities. Physically, the reasonable person resembles the defendant. In other words, if the defendant is blind, the standard would be: "Did the defendant do what a reasonable blind person would have done in the same circumstances?" If the defendant is deaf, the standard would be the actions of a reasonable deaf person, and so on.

Interviewer: Suppose the defendant was under the influence of drugs or alcohol. What would the standard be then?

Mr. Cohen: Well, no allowances are made for people using alcohol or drugs. They're still held to the standard of the reasonable sober person — not the reasonable drunk or drug taker.

Interviewer: Let's get back to how the reasonable person acts.

Mr. Cohen: All right. The reasonable person is expected to have a certain level of knowledge. For example, on a very simple level, he is assumed to know that if he tosses a rock from a window, it will fall. And he should also know that if he placed a rock on a window ledge seven stories up, it might fall and hurt someone below. The reasonable person therefore would use care to make certain that the rock does not cause damage. In fact, the reasonable person probably would not put the rock on the sill in the first place.

Interviewer: But suppose you

honestly didn't know something that a reasonable person was expected to know. Could you still be found negligent?

Mr. Cohen: You certainly could! The reasonable person has a duty to find out what he does not know so that he can meet the standard of minimum knowledge. And that standard can be quite high in this day of advanced technology.

Interviewer: Can you give an example?

Mr. Cohen: Suppose a worn tire blew out on your car causing you to lose control and hit a pedestrian. You could be found negligent for not having replaced the tire. If you said that you didn't know the tire was worn or that a worn tire was dangerous, your ignorance probably would not be an excuse. As a driver, it is your duty to know about the condition of your car and to find out about the dangers of such things as worn tires or faulty steering.

Interviewer: Well, I can see that if you were an auto mechanic . . .

Mr. Cohen: Ah now, if you were an auto mechanic, you would be a person of special knowledge and special skills. And you would be expected to meet a higher standard. You would be held to the standard of other auto mechanics. Suppose it was your own personal judgment that your tires were safe, but it was the opinion of the average mechanic that they were extremely dangerous. You would most certainly be found negligent. In the same way, a doctor or lawyer is held to the standard of knowledge and care expected of the reasonable doctor or lawyer.

Interviewer: It seems a terribly rigid standard. After all, suppose a doctor is treating a lot of people in a highway smashup in a heavy rainstorm. This is very different from dealing with just one patient in a hospital.

Mr. Cohen: In a negligence suit, the judge or jury considers all of the circumstances before deciding on the actions of the reasonable person. For instance, if the suit arises from a traffic accident, weather, traffic, and road conditions are taken into account. Or if the situation involves an emergency, that too is taken into account. These things may alter somewhat the court's idea of the reasonable person.

Interviewer: It seems that if people

just use good common sense and try to anticipate the consequences of their actions before taking them, they should be fairly safe.

Mr. Cohen: That's probably true in many cases. But there's one important difference between the reasonable person and those of us who are flesh and blood. We often lose our temper or act emotionally. The reasonable person doesn't have such weaknesses. He or she is *always* reasonable!

Your Turn

1. Do you think the "reasonable person" is a fair standard to apply in negligence cases? Why?

2. Some important questions about the Neece/Turner case were left unanswered. See if you can answer them, using the standard of the reasonable person.

   a. Did Dan Turner have a duty to use care?

   b. Do you think he used or failed to use proper care?

Reaching a decision

In the Neece/Turner case, Dan did have a duty to use care. As we have just seen in the interview with Arnold Cohen, people who drive are expected to take reasonable precautions. They must check for safety both in the condition of their car and in the way they drive.

Did Dan use proper care? On the facts given, courts might differ on their decisions. But further information might point more clearly to an answer.

For example, suppose the seat lock had come loose the week before when Dan was driving. "I must get that fixed," he'd said—but then forgot all about it. In this case, the reasonable person would know that the seat could shift again and cause an accident. Dan would probably be found negligent.

On the other hand, suppose the car was brand new. Before taking it out, Dan had set the seat to a comfortable position and then pushed it to make sure it was locked. The reasonable person could hardly do more to take proper care.

In this case, however, there could still be negligence. Instead of Dan, the automobile manufacturer or dealer might be held liable. We will disc___ kind of liability on a late___

2. Is it reasonable?

Every day people find themselves in situations where they have to decide whether or not to take chances. There's no time to think over all the possible consequences. Other times the risk doesn't seem important enough to worry about. And most of the time, things work out with little or no harm done to anyone. Once in a while, however, this kind of decision can end up as a lawsuit.

Look at each of the situations below. Consider what you would do in each. Then decide what you think the standard of the "reasonable person" would be in each situation.

1. You are walking your dog when you meet a friend who's also walking a dog. Suddenly, the two dogs break away from you and begin to fight viciously. You feel you would be bitten if you tried to stop the fight with your bare hands. You look around and see a long stick lying in the street.
• What do you think you would (or would not) do?
• What do you think the

"reasonable person" would do under the same circumstances?

2. You are driving along the street in your car. You stop at a stop sign. A stranger jumps into your car. He is waving a gun and tells you to drive on. You don't know if he would really use the gun or not, but you obey. Then you start thinking. You have seen this man's face and he knows you could identify him later. You're afraid he may kill you unless you can get away from him.

• What do you think you would (or would not) do?

• What do you think the "reasonable person" would do under the same circumstances?

3. You have found an old golf club and a golf ball in the hall closet. You take them into the backyard. Your six-year-old brother and a friend are in one corner of the yard so you go to the other corner. You hit the ball a couple of times and the phone rings. You wonder whether to leave the club and ball in the backyard while you're on the phone. After all, you will be coming back out in a few minutes.

• What do you think you would (or would not) do?

• What do you think the "reasonable person" would do under the same circumstances?

136

Your Turn

The three situations you just read are based on actual court cases. These cases are described below. If you were a judge or a member of a jury, how would you decide each case? Use the questions below to guide you in reaching a decision. Then write a paragraph explaining each decision.

• What action did the defendant take (or fail to take)?

• Do you think the defendant had a duty to use care?

• What do you think a reasonable person would have done in the same situation? Do you think the defendant met the standard of the reasonable person?

• Did the plaintiff suffer damages?

• Was the defendant's action (or failure to act) the cause of the plaintiff's damage?

• Do you think the defendant was negligent?

Brown v. Kendall

Mr. Brown's and Mr. Kendall's dogs were fighting. Kendall picked up a stick and tried to break up the fight. At this point Brown was standing close behind him. As Kendall swung the stick at the dogs, he accidently struck Brown in the eye. Brown sued Kendall for negligence.

Cordas v. Peerless Transportation Co.

Mr. Cordas robbed a store and wanted to make a quick getaway. He jumped into a taxi owned by the Peerless Transportation Company and ordered the driver to move. The driver was frightened but did as he was told. He drove a short distance, then slammed on the brakes and jumped out of the car. The car, still in gear, kept going and went over a curb, injuring Cordas. Cordas later sued the taxi company for negligence.

Lubitz v. Wells

Mr. Wells enjoyed playing golf. He sometimes practiced in his backyard. One day he left the club in the yard. His small son picked up the club to try and hit a rock with it. As the child swung, he hit a neighbor's child in the jaw by mistake. The neighbor sued Wells for negligence in leaving the club in the yard.

Ask your teacher for the results of the three cases. They are on pages 37 and 38 of the teaching guide.

Simulation: *Neece v. Turner*

Invite an attorney specializing in torts to visit the classroom and to act as judge for the mock trial.

Before the visit, choose various members of the class to play the parts of: court officer; court reporter; attorneys for the Neece family; attorneys for the Turner family; Howie Neece; Tommy Neece; Dan and Evelyn Turner.

In preparing the case, attorneys for the Neece family must show:

1. Dan Turner took (or failed to take) an action;

2. Dan Turner had a duty to use care and failed to use the proper care;

3. the Neeces suffered damages by the injury to Tommy;

4. what Dan Turner did (or failed to do) caused the damages suffered by the Neeces.

Attorneys for the Turners should try to show that:

1. Dan Turner did exercise the care of a reasonable person;

2. the damage would be unavoidable by the average reasonable person under the same circumstances.

After the case has been heard and the decision has been reached, discuss the outcome with the attorney who played the judge.

3.
Minors and negligence

We've talked about the standard of the reasonable person as it applies to adults. But what about minors?

Suppose, for example, that a six-year-old child left a skateboard at the foot of a flight of stairs in an apartment building. An elderly man coming down the stairs slips on it, falls and breaks his hip. Should the adult standard apply?

Or suppose it was a 15-year-old girl who left the skateboard. Would that make a difference? Should a 15-year-old minor be held to the same standard of behavior as a reasonable adult?

In the past, under common law, children under the age of seven were not held responsible for their actions. They were thought not to have enough experience to make reasoned judgment. Even children between the ages of seven and fourteen were generally thought incapable of negligence.

Today, however, these age limits do not apply in most courts. Now, children are usually held to the standard of behavior of a reasonable child of similar age and experience.

What would this mean in a case like the skateboard injury? A court would consider whether children of similar age and experience would be able to foresee the dangers of leaving a skateboard at the foot of a flight of stairs. If so, the child could be found negligent.

Your Turn

1. Suppose you were deciding the skateboard case. Would you find the six-year-old negligent in view of the reasonable standard of a normal six-year-old? What about the 15-year-old?

2. At what age should a person be judged by the standard of a "reasonable adult"? Why?

Story No. 1

One day 14-year-old James was walking home from school when he saw something in the bushes. He took a closer look and saw that it was an old rusted air gun. He picked it up and tucked it inside his coat. He stopped at the store and bought a package of "BB's."

When he got home he went out to the alley in back of his apartment. He oiled the gun and filled it with the "BB's." He was just about to fire it when he heard his mother call him in to dinner. He didn't want to take the gun because he was afraid she wouldn't let him keep it. He set it down next to the alley fence and

crumpled some old newspapers over it to hide it. Then he went inside.

A few minutes later, James and his mother heard screaming. They went outside to see what had happened. Seven-year-old Mike from next door had found the gun and pulled the trigger, thinking it was a toy. The "BB's" had gone into his leg and it was bleeding badly.

Story No. 2

One day 14-year-old James was walking home from school when he saw something in the bushes. He took a closer look and saw that it was an old rusted air gun. He picked it up and tucked it inside his coat. He stopped at the store and bought a package of "BB's."

When he got home he went out to the alley in back of his apartment. He oiled the gun and filled it with the "BB's." He was just about to fire it when his mother came outside to call him to dinner.

"Where on earth did you get that gun?" his mother asked in horror.

"Oh, mom," James said, "it's just an old air gun. I'll be careful with it."

"Not in my house you won't," she said. "I'm not having any

140

guns in here. You find someplace safe to put it and then you come on up to dinner." His mother went back inside.

James set the gun down next to the alley fence and crumpled some old newspapers over it to hide it. Then he went inside.

A few minutes later, James and his mother heard screaming. They went outside to see what had happened. Seven-year-old Mike from next door had found the gun and pulled the trigger. The "BB's" had gone into his leg and it was bleeding badly.

Your Turn

1. How are the two stories alike? How are they different?

2. Do you think James was negligent in either of the two stories? Do you think his mother was negligent in either story?

When parents are responsible

As a general rule, parents are not held responsible for the negligent acts of their children. There is one important exception, however. That is if parents are aware of a dangerous situation involving their children and allow it to continue. Thus parents may be held responsible if they allow their children to have things which may become dangerous to others. In some cases, parents may be held responsible just because they have left such things within reach of their children.

In the first story, therefore, James's mother probably would not be held responsible for his negligence. She didn't know that James had the air gun. In the second story, however, she might very well be held responsible. She knew that James had the air gun and allowed him to keep it. She told him to put it in a safe place but didn't exercise proper care in seeing that he did so.

If the parents are held responsible for a child's negligence, obviously they have to pay any damages. But what happens if the child is held responsible?

In that case, damages must be paid out of money belonging to the child. Most children, of course, own very little money. However, judgments in negligence cases are good for ten years. In other words, money earned by or given to the child for ten years may be used to pay the damages.

Your Turn

Read the following case study. Then write your answers to the questions which follow.

Horton v. Pittsburg Reduction Co.

The Pittsburg Reduction Company threw away some dynamite caps in an area where neighborhood children often played. Thirteen-year-old Charlie Copple found some of the caps and took them home. His parents looked at the caps and thought they were "shells of some kind." They let Charlie keep them and play with them. A week later Charlie took them to school and traded them to another 13-year-old boy named Horton. The Horton boy noticed some dirt in the caps and tried to dig it out with a match. The cap exploded, maiming his hand.

1. Was there a duty to use care on the part of the Pittsburg Reduction Co.? Charlie Copple? His parents? Horton? Should a 13-year-old boy be aware of the dangers involved in playing with dynamite caps?

2. The Horton family sued the Pittsburg Reduction Co. for negligence in disposing of the caps. The company argued that the injury to Horton was caused by the negligence of Charlie's parents, who allowed him to keep them. Who do you think should be held responsible? Write a paragraph explaining your answer.

142

Ask your teacher for the result of this case. It is listed on page 38 of the teaching guide.

4.
Cars and negligence

In some cases, courts may judge minors by the standard not of a reasonable child but of a reasonable adult. This happens when the minor is involved in a normal adult activity. For example, a minor who drives a car or boat, or flies an airplane, may be expected to meet the adult standard of care. Youth or inexperience may not be a defense.

Fernando's new car

Fernando had completed his drivers' education class at school and had just gotten his first driver's license. He wanted a car more than anything. He didn't have much money—just what he had saved from summer work as a carpenter's apprentice. He had nearly $400. Naturally he was thrilled when he found a ten-year-old pick-up truck for $350.

Fernando bought the car, registered it with the Department of Motor Vehicles and then took it home to check it out. The previous owner had told him that the brakes needed to be replaced. Other than that the car seemed to be in good shape.

Fernando called a couple of insurance companies to find out about insurance rates. He found them to be very high. He didn't have nearly enough money. Fernando was very disappointed. He knew that he shouldn't drive without insurance but he hadn't even had a chance to show the car to his friends. He decided to drive it just that one afternoon.

He drove slowly over to his friend Jeff's house. Wanda, Jeff's girlfriend, was also there. They both wanted to ride in Fernando's new car. He told them the car needed new brakes, but the friends wanted to take a short ride anyway. They all crowded into the front of the pick-up truck.

"Have you opened it up to see what it'll do?" Wanda asked.

"No," Fernando answered. "I don't want to do that until I get the brakes fixed."

"Oh, come on," Jeff urged. "Just take it up to 60, anyway."

Fernando hesitated. He looked around the street—no traffic and no people. He decided to take it up to 60 for just a moment. He did. The car accelerated like a dream.

"Fantastic!" Jeff yelled.

Then Fernando saw a stop sign at the end of the street. He stepped on the brakes but nothing happened.

"Put on the handbrake!" Wanda shouted.

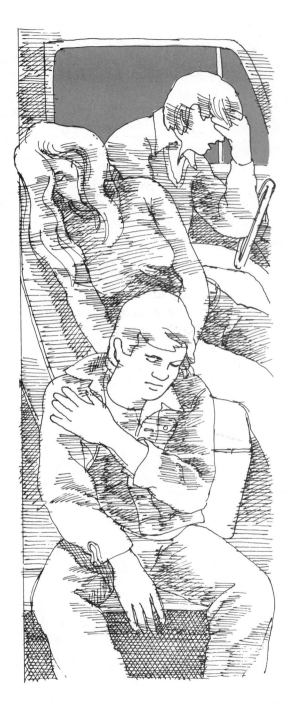

Fernando pulled on the handbrake just as the pick-up reached the intersection. But it was too late. A car was already coming across from the left. There was a loud crash as Fernando plowed into the side of a new station wagon.

When Fernando recovered from the impact, he looked around. Wanda was unconscious. Her head had hit the windshield and there was a trickle of blood from a gash in her forehead. Jeff was moaning and holding his shoulder.

The new station wagon was in terrible shape. A crowd of people had begun to gather and some were talking to the woman driving the station wagon. She said that her back hurt and she was dizzy.

Your Turn

1. Do you think the driver of the station wagon has grounds for a negligence action against Fernando? Why?

2. Do you think that Fernando should be held to the standard of the reasonable adult? Why?

The outcome

If a suit were brought against Fernando, the court would probably hold him to an adult standard. The driver of the station wagon could sue Fernando for her injuries and for property damage to her car. She might also ask for damages for pain and inconvenience. If she were unable to work for a time, she could sue him for loss of income. And if she were permanently disabled, she could sue for loss of future income. On top of all that, she might ask for punitive damages. These are sometimes awarded when there has been "gross" negligence — that is, when the defendant has behaved recklessly or has taken foolish chances. In this case, the plaintiff might charge that Fernando was grossly or recklessly negligent because he knew his brakes were in poor condition but still drove fast.

In other words, if Fernando were found negligent, he might have to pay heavy damages. The amount would depend upon the decision of the court. But it could run into thousands or even tens of thousands of dollars.

Where would Fernando get the money? If he had had insurance, this probably would have covered most or all of the damages. But without insurance, Fernando would have to pay the damages himself. His car could be taken to help pay and so could any other property he owns. What is more,

the judgment is good for ten years. During that time, a portion of his earnings could be taken each month until the debt is paid.

Your Turn

1. If you were a judge hearing this case, do you think you would find Fernando negligent? Grossly negligent? Not negligent? Why?

2. Suppose Fernando's friends bring suit against him for their injuries. Do you think he should be held responsible? Should the fact that they knew about the condition of the brakes before getting into the car be taken into account? Should the fact that they encouraged Fernando to "see what it'll do" be taken into account? Why?

Resource person. Invite a local attorney who specializes in personal injury cases to visit your class. Ask the attorney to talk with you about the laws in your state regarding the liability of drivers and owners of automobiles. Before the visit, prepare a list of questions you would like to discuss. Your list might include:

1. If you are driving your parents' car and you cause an accident, who is liable? You or your parents?

2. If a friend has insurance and

is driving your car, who is liable if the friend causes an accident?

3. If you wreck a friend's car and the friend has insurance even though you do not, will you have to pay or will the damage be covered by your friend's insurance?

4. Is there "no-fault" insurance in your state? If so, how does that affect your personal liability?

5. Is insurance required by law in your state? What can happen if you cause an accident and don't have insurance?

5.
Strict liability

In the cases we have talked about so far, the defendants were liable for damages only if they were found negligent. But there are some cases which involve what is called *strict liability*. In these cases, the person bringing suit need not prove negligence or intention to win damages.

When and how does strict liability apply? Let's look first at two different cases involving pets.

Susan's dog
Susan's dog was big and friendly. He was a favorite to all the neighborhood kids. Usually Susan kept him in the yard because she lived on a busy street.

One day a visitor left the front gate open and the dog got out. Susan wasn't too alarmed when she noticed that he was gone. He had gotten out before. Usually he ran up the street and then came back home.

Some time later, Susan heard yelling in the street. She ran outside to see what was the matter. There was a woman holding the seat of her pants, shouting that Susan's dog had bitten her.

Susan was shocked. "But he's never bitten anyone in his life!"

"Well, he sure did bite her," one of the neighbor kids said to another with a little giggle. "I saw him do it."

Anna's dog

Anna lived alone in an area where the crime rate was very high. She bought a Doberman to protect her and her property. She worked with the dog and trained him well—too well.

One afternoon, a friend came by to show Anna a new blouse.

"Just look at this," the friend said as she pulled out the blouse with a quick flourish.

The dog growled and jumped for her arm. He had bitten her before Anna could pull him off.

The friend wasn't seriously hurt and didn't take any action. After that, Anna warned her friends not to make any sudden moves when the dog was around.

One evening when Anna came home from work, she failed to latch the gate. The dog got out. Anna went out to look for him as soon as she found he was missing.

The search didn't take long. She heard screams and ran toward them. She found her dog standing over a small boy who had been bitten badly on the face and neck.

Your Turn

1. Do you think Susan should be liable for the injury caused by her dog? Do you think Anna should be liable for the injury caused by *her* dog?

2. What differences are there between the two cases? Do you think these should make a difference to the liability? Why?

The outcome

Pet owners may be held strictly liable for any injuries caused by their animals. In other words, it makes no difference whether the owner was or was not negligent.

Under common law, there is one exception. Pet owners are held strictly liable only if they know that the pet is dangerous. Dogs are entitled to "one free bite." In other words, a dog owner cannot be expected to know that his or her pet is dangerous unless the dog has shown that it is. So

147

under common law, Susan probably would not be held strictly liable for her dog's first bite.

However, in recent years, many communities have passed laws doing away with the "one bite" rule. In these communities pet owners are strictly liable for *all* damage or injury caused by their pets. If Susan lived in one of these communities, she would be held strictly liable even though she didn't know her dog was dangerous.

As for Anna, she knew that her dog was dangerous because he had bitten someone before. So she would be held strictly liable even under common law. She was also negligent in failing to latch the gate. But the victim or his parents would not have to prove this in order to recover damages.

Turn back to page 128 and look at the five points that a plaintiff has to prove in order to claim damages for negligence. In cases of strict liability, the plaintiff does not have to prove points 2 and 3. He or she does not have to prove that the defendant had a duty to use care but failed to.

Injuries caused by pets make up an important area of strict liability. However, strict liability also applies in other types of cases. Let's look at some.

Dangerous activities

People can be held strictly liable for any damages they cause if they are carrying out unusually hazardous or dangerous activities. How dangerous must it be?

Siegler v. Kuhlman

Aaron Kuhlman was hauling gasoline in a truck trailer on a freeway. Somehow the trailer broke loose from a cab, went through a chain link fence, and landed on the street below. A 17-year-old girl, Carol Houseman, was driving on the street below and ran into the trailer. The gasoline exploded and Carol's car caught fire. She was killed.

Carol's guardian, Mr. Siegler,

sued Kuhlman for damages. The court ruled that hauling gasoline was a dangerous activity and that Kuhlman was strictly liable for Carol's death. He had to pay heavy damages.

Product safety

As you saw in Part One, the legal protection of consumers has increased steadily in recent years. This includes protection from unsafe products. If a consumer suffers damages from any product that is shown to be defective or dangerous, the seller may be held strictly liable.

Here are two examples of suits brought on the grounds of strict product liability:

Cronin v. J. B. Olson Corp.

The J. B. Olson Corp. had a special order from a bread company to provide several vans with built-in bread racks. The racks were designed to slide forward and backward and also to lock into a fixed position. Mr. Cronin, a driver for the bread company, was driving one of the vans when he had an accident. The impact of the crash broke the metal clasp which held the bread racks in place. The trays were thrust forward with such force that they pushed the driver through the windshield. He filed suit on the grounds of strict liability. He claimed that the clasp holding the trays was defective.

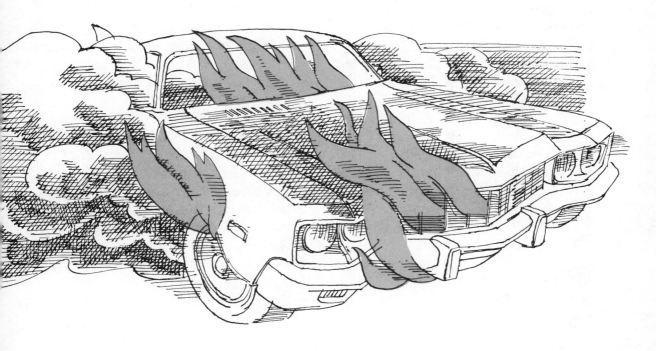

Your Turn

1. Do you think that the J. B. Olson Corp. should have reasonably "foreseen" that an accident might occur and taken that into account in designing the clasp? Why?

2. Would you hold the J. B. Olson Corp. strictly liable if you were deciding the case? Why?

McDevitt v. Standard Oil Co. of Texas

Mr. McDevitt bought five tires from a Standard station in Texas. The station attendant told him that the tires were the wrong size and type for his car. McDevitt said he wanted the tires anyway, and the attendant made the sale. When the tires were put on his car, he did not inflate them according to the instructions. He drove the car hard—sometimes at high speeds and on dirt roads. One day, while driving with his family, a tire blew out. This caused an accident which injured his wife and children. McDevitt sued Standard Oil Co. of Texas on the grounds of strict liability.

Your Turn

1. The dealer warned the buyer that the tires would not meet the use to which Mr. McDevitt wished

150

to put them. Do you think that should relieve Standard Oil of strict liability?

2. If you were a judge hearing this case would you decide in favor of McDevitt or in favor of Standard Oil of Texas? Why?

Ask your teacher for the results of these two cases. They are listed on page 39 of the teaching guide.

Resource person. Check back to the list of consumer agencies in your community that you prepared for the unit on Consumer Law. Invite a member of one of these agencies to visit your classroom to discuss product liability. Before the visit, prepare a list of questions you would like to ask. These might include:

1. Can you give some examples of actions that have been brought in our community on the grounds of strict product liability? How were these cases decided?

2. If there is a notice limiting liability on a product at the time it is purchased, does that mean that the manufacturer cannot be held strictly liable if the product turns out to be defective or unsafe?

3. Generally, does misusing a product or altering it in some way remove the burden of strict liability from the seller? Why?

Chapter 10

Mostly Deliberate

In Chapter Nine we followed the story of Dan Turner and Tommy Neece's broken arm. That was an unintentional tort. Dan had not meant to hit the bike and harm Tommy.

But suppose things had happened differently, and Dan had meant to hit the bike. Now Tommy's father could sue Dan for an intentional tort. He would probably ask for punitive damages in addition to payment for the injury.

There are widely differing types of intentional torts. For example, suppose a person tries to harm someone else and fails. As we'll see in a moment, that can still be an intentional tort. Or suppose a person takes an action which he or she thinks is harmless, but it turns out to damage someone else. That, too, may count as an intentional tort.

In this chapter we will look at some of the most common types of intentional wrongs. These are assault, battery, trespass, libel, and slander.

1.
Assault

Here is one of the earliest assault cases on record:

In the year 1348 in England, a man came to a tavern to buy some wine. He was carrying a hatchet. When he found the tavern closed, he used the handle of the hatchet to pound on the door. After a time, the tavern keeper's wife came to a window and leaned out. She told the man that the tavern was closed and was going to stay closed, so he should stop pounding. With this, the man swung his hatchet at the woman. He missed, but her husband took him to court. The man was found guilty of assault.

For there to be an assault, one person must do something to another person which causes that person to fear immediate and unpleasant contact. This action must be taken without the second person's consent.

As you can see, there can be assault without any actual harm—just the immediate threat of contact. However, words alone don't usually make an assault. There must be some kind of action as well. For example, suppose someone walked up to you and said, "I'm going to beat you up."

This would probably not be considered an assault unless that person also made some move to carry out the threat. The threat would not be immediate until that person, say, raised his fist to swing at you. If the person did take a swing, it would be an assault whether the fist connected or not.

In Chapter Nine, we said you could *not* sue for damages if a car was coming straight at you but you jumped out of the way in time. But there we were talking about an accident, or an unintentional threat. In that case, you could sue only for harm actually suffered. But if the driver of the car deliberately aimed at you, the picture changes. Then you could sue even if you were unhurt. You would have suffered assault.

Now look at the following story:

Gun practice

Nineteen-year-old Mary had just returned from a hunting trip with her family and was helping her father clean the guns. First they made certain that all the guns were empty. Then they cleaned and oiled them. When they were through, Mary decided to take one of the empty guns into the backyard to practice sighting.

As she was taking aim, a neighbor, Mr. Merriweather, looked over the backyard fence.

"Hey, is that thing real?" he asked nervously.

"Sure is," said Mary. Seeing the fear in Mr. Merriweather's face, she decided to have a little fun. Putting a villainous smile on her face, Mary turned the gun toward Mr. Merriweather. Carefully she took aim.

Mr. Merriweather stood rooted in fear.

Holding the gun steady, Mary slowly pulled the trigger. There was a click.

"Bang, you're dead!" Mary laughed. "Bet I scared you, huh, Mr. Merriweather?" She laughed again as she lowered the gun.

Mr. Merriweather was not amused.

Your Turn

Do you think Mary committed an assault or not? Give your reasons.

The court's view

If Mr. Merriweather charged Mary with assault, he would very likely win. It makes no difference that Mary never intended to shoot him or even that the gun was empty. The fact is that she made Mr. Merriweather believe she was going to shoot him. He was in fear

of immediate harm and therefore had cause for a suit against her.

Action Project

Divide the class into groups of two to three people. Then work with your group to create a situation, other than those described in the book, which illustrates an assault. Ask each group to act out its situation and then discuss what took place. Use the following questions as a basis for discussion:

1. Did one party take an action?
2. What was the purpose of that action?
3. Did the other party suffer fear of immediate harm or undesirable contact?
4. Did the first party's action cause that fear?
5. Was there an assault? Why?

2. Battery

The Prince was so overcome when he saw Sleeping Beauty that he knelt down and gently kissed her face. Sleeping Beauty's eyelids fluttered open. She saw the prince standing by her side. Then . . .

1. "Thank you, my prince," Beauty said softly. "Your kiss has awakened me from my long sleep. You are my true love."

2. "Yecch!" Beauty yelled. "How dare you kiss me! I never would have let you do it in a million years if I'd been awake. And you knew that. You always were a creep and you always will be! Yecch!"

Is a kiss a battery? In ending No. 2 it is and in No. 1 it is not. A battery is *any* contact with another person which is made without consent and is harmful or offensive to that person.

The term "battery" comes from a French word that means "beating," and in most cases the contact is more violent than a kiss. Often, assault and battery go together. One person threatens to punch another person and takes a swing. That is assault. He connects. That is battery.

Serious cases of assault or battery or both may be considered criminal offenses. This may happen, for example, if extreme violence is involved, or if a person commits the assault or battery while carrying out another crime. In such cases the state will prosecute the offender. However, the victim can still bring a civil action against the offender for damages.

A person can commit a battery

even without making direct contact with someone else's body.

Fisher v. Carrousel Motor Hotel, Inc.

Mr. Fisher, a black man, went to dinner at a private club that had a rule against serving blacks. While Fisher was standing in the buffet line, the manager of the club walked up to him and jerked the plate from his hand. Fisher was not physically hurt, in fear of being hurt, or even touched by the manager. However, he felt humiliated and he sued the club for battery. The court agreed that battery had taken place and awarded him damages.

This case depended on the manager's motive. In grabbing the plate, he intended to be insulting or offensive to Fisher. When a person has that motive, contact with another person's body, clothing, or even something he or she is holding or touching can be a battery. And the person committing the battery can also be held responsible for any unintended results of the action. For example, the manager intended only to grab the plate from Fisher's hand. However, if the plate had broken and it had cut Fisher, the manager could be held responsible for the injury.

Minors and battery

As children play games, throw things, and quarrel, they make contact with other persons more often than most adults do. When do such contacts count as battery?

In Chapter Nine we saw how the standard of the "reasonable child" is used in accidental torts. In battery cases, too, a minor is held to the standard of children of similar age and experience. In other words, a minor must have enough experience to be able to foresee the results of the action before he or she can be held responsible for a battery.

For example, suppose a two-year-old boy pulled a curtain rod down on the head of a visitor to his home. He probably would not have the age and experience to foresee the results of the action. But suppose a 10-year-old did the same thing. If he pulled the rod down deliberately and could reasonably foresee that it might fall on the visitor, he might be liable for battery.

When are parents responsible?

As with negligent torts, parents usually are not held responsible for batteries committed by their children. However, they may become liable if they tell the child to carry out the act or give permission to do so, or if their negligence makes the act possible.

The babysitter

Betty, a 15-year-old high school student, had a violent temper from the time she was a small child. Even her parents were sometimes frightened by her rages.

Luckily Betty didn't lose her temper very often. Most of her friends and neighbors were not aware of her problem.

When Mrs. Alonso down the street called Betty to ask her to babysit for her seven-year-old son, Betty was pleased. She would have the chance to make some extra money. Her mother was a little concerned. After all, she did worry about what might happen if the child angered Betty. But Betty hadn't had a temper flare-up for quite a while, and she thought the responsibility of babysitting might be good for Betty. She told Betty that she could babysit.

The babysitting job seemed to go fine at first. Betty fixed dinner for Tommy, let him watch TV for a while, and then put him to bed. She had just started on her homework when he was out of bed again. Patiently Betty told him to get back in bed. A few minutes later, there he was at the door again. Time after time it happened.

Betty could feel her face getting very hot. Suddenly she was filled with rage. She picked up her binder and threw it at him. The corner of the binder struck him just above the eye, leaving a large gash.

Your Turn

Do you think that Betty's parents should be held responsible for her actions? Why?

Resource Person. Invite someone from your community who specializes in the legal problems of juveniles—for example, a social worker or probation officer. Ask your guest to talk with your class about some of the assault and battery cases involving minors that have occurred in your community. Ask your guest to discuss with you the conditions under which simple assault and battery becomes criminal assault and battery and what can happen if someone is sued in a civil action and charged with a crime as well.

3.
Trespass

Hazel and Jenny decided it would be nice to get out of the city for the day. The two friends packed a picnic lunch, checked the tires on their bikes and took off toward the hills.

The country roads were lovely. It was late autumn and the leaves on the trees were bright yellow, red, and orange. After they had ridden for almost two hours, they decided to stop for their picnic. They left their bicycles locked to a tree and walked toward a small stream running through an open field.

They unpacked their basket, unrolled a small blanket, and sat down for a relaxing lunch. Hazel had taken only one bite of her sandwich when she heard a rustling in the grass behind them. She turned around to see a man in coveralls standing close by.

"What do you think you're doing?" he called.

"We're having a picnic. Why?" Hazel called back.

"Well, this is my land and you're trespassing. I want you out of here now!"

The man's attitude made Hazel angry. They weren't causing any harm. "We'll leave when we're good and ready to," Hazel said.

"If you know what's good for you, you'll get out now!" the man shouted. "Or else I'll take stronger measures!"

"Oh go away," Jenny muttered.

A question of intent

There are different kinds of trespass, but the most common is trespass on land. This happens when someone goes onto another person's land without permission.

If a person deliberately goes onto property that is legally occupied by someone else, that person is liable for trespass. Jenny and Hazel intended to be on the land even though they didn't know it was privately owned. This makes them liable for a trespass action.

Suppose a friend had given them permission to picnic on his land and they had gone to the wrong property by mistake. Would they still be liable for trespass? Yes. Their reasons for being on the land are usually of no concern in a trespass action. The important point is that they went onto the land of their own free will. If someone had physically pushed them onto the land, they would not be liable for trespass.

In cases where there is no

actual damage to the property, the court usually awards a small amount, such as six cents and court costs. (Note that these costs often run somewhere from two to 100 dollars or more.) You might be wondering why anyone would sue someone for six cents. But there may be a very good reason. Even if a trespass does no harm to the property, it may damage the owner's rights. Suppose an owner allows people to trespass on his property without taking any action. The owner may be considered to have given consent, and after a certain time he or she may lose the right to exclusive possession of the property. Therefore, people often bring trespass suits simply to protect their rights.

"Stronger measures"

How far may a person go in trying to keep trespassers off his or her property, or in trying to remove them once they are there? Is a property owner allowed to use force?

Here is a case which centers around those questions:

Katko v. Briney

Mrs. Briney inherited a farmhouse. Since she and her husband had another home, they never lived on the inherited property. They used the farmhouse to store a collection of antique bottles. They boarded up the doors and windows and posted "No trespassing" signs. Even so, the house was broken into several times and bottles were stolen.

The Brineys were fed up with the constant burglarizing and decided to put a stop to it. Mr. Briney set up a shotgun in the bedroom of the farmhouse. He carefully rigged it so that whoever opened the door would trigger the gun.

A man by the name of Katko entered the house. He intended to take some bottles—just as he had done in the past. When he opened the bedroom door, the shotgun fired and blew off most of Katko's leg.

Katko sued the Brineys. The court ruled that the value of human life is greater than that of property. It pointed out that neither Mr. nor Mrs. Briney was in any danger from Katko, and therefore they had no right to set up the booby trap. The Brineys had to pay Katko damages for injury and punitive damages as well.

Reasonable force

If people are trespassing on your property, you may use a certain amount of force to remove them. The general rule is that you may use only as much force as is reasonable under the circumstances. In the picnic story, for example, the owner could have taken Jenny and Hazel by the arm and led them off his land.

However, you do not have the right to hurt a trespasser unless he or she is threatening you with physical harm and is able to carry out that threat. In other words, you or your family must be in danger of immediate harm before you may use extreme or deadly force. Otherwise you may be liable to a suit for damages, or even for criminal charges.

Action Project

Divide the class into groups of four or five students. Have each group discuss the following issues and reach a majority decision on the questions raised.

1. Only the person who occupies the land can sue for trespass. This means that if a property owner rents to a tenant who occupies the property, only the tenant can sue for trespass—not the landlord. Often landlords retain the right to make reasonable inspections of their property from time to time. But suppose a landlord goes beyond the bounds of reasonable inspections and enters your home whenever he or she feels like it. Would you have the right to file suit against the landlord for trespass?

2. Under common law, the occupier of land had rights not only to the surface but to all the land below it to the center of the earth and to all the air above it extending to infinity. Do you think that these rights should still hold good today? For example, should people who live in the path of an airport be able to sue airlines for trespass? Should the altitude at which planes pass over the property be taken into account? Should the question of whether the occupier of the land or the airport was there first be considered? Why?

3. Should trespass actions be limited to the presence of people on another's land or should it extend to things as well? For example, suppose someone is shooting a gun on his own property but the bullets fly across your property. Should that person be liable for trespass? Why?

161

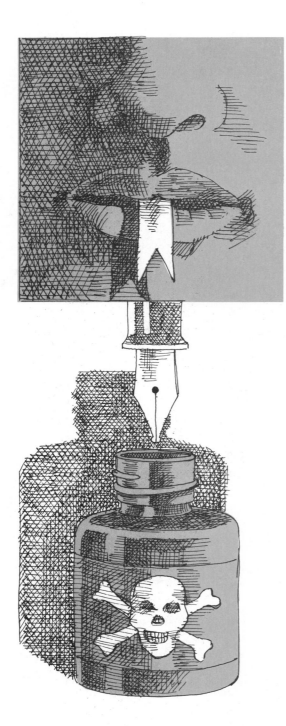

4.
Libel and slander

"Congratulations, Joan," Larry said sarcastically. "You got quite a promotion. I guess your bosses don't know that you're a liar and a cheat. You're ripping this store off right and left. I know it, and it's time other people knew it, too."

Does Larry have the right to say this about Joan? That all depends. If it's true, he has the right to say it to anyone. But suppose it's not true. If Larry tells this to her in front of her bosses and they fire Joan as a result, she may have cause for action. She might sue Larry for slander.

Both slander and libel consist of spreading false information about a person and thus causing damage to that person. Slander refers to spoken information, libel to written or printed information. Today, libel usually includes false information given on radio or television, even if spoken.

A person suing for slander or libel must show three things:
• First, as we've seen, that the information is false.
• Second, that the false information was spread—that is, communicated to at least one other person. If Larry had made his speech to Joan when they

were alone in a closed elevator, there would be no slander. But if he shouted it when the elevator doors opened on a busy floor, then he would be spreading the information to other people.

• Third, that the false information has caused damage. Suppose someone goes around saying that you were born in Chicago and play the piano, when in fact you were born in Seattle and have no ear for music. This false information in itself is not damaging. However, if it makes people think that *you* are a liar, you may then have grounds for a slander action. Damage can include lowering the reputation of the person, or losing the companionship of those who have heard the information. In Joan's case, she might also prove that Larry's slander caused her to lose her job.

False information usually reaches more people when it is printed or broadcast than when it is spoken. As a result, damages awarded for libel are sometimes extremely high. However, awards can vary considerably, depending on the facts of each case. Suppose Joan could prove that Larry knew the information was false and was deliberately trying to harm her. In that case, she might also win

punitive or "punishment" damages.

Slander and libel can be costly to the defendant. If Joan won her case, she could be awarded money for damage to her reputation, loss of companionship and loss of income, and also for punitive damages. The total award could run into several thousand dollars.

Your Turn

Make up one example each of a slanderous statement and a libelous statement. Show how each meets the three requirements listed above.

How free can free speech be?

In this age of TV, radio, newspapers, and magazines, the laws of libel raise some difficult issues. The news media are constantly pouring forth information about people—that is their business. Suppose they make an honest mistake and publish false information which they believe to be true? This story is an example:

June's juicy gossip

June Tanaka wrote the gossip column for her school newspaper. She never wrote anything that would hurt anybody—just tidbits

about who was dating whom, who wore what to the school dances, and so on.

One afternoon after school, June and several of her friends went to the coffee shop across the street to talk about the day's events. She noticed another group of students sitting at a nearby table. She saw the waitress bring a tray of steaming cups of coffee and doughnuts to their table. Quickly Jane noted their names and what they were eating. A good item for her column.

Next week, June's column came out in the school paper. One of the items read as follows: "Spotted pretty Nancy Lyons, among others, drinking coffee and devouring doughnuts at Biffy's Restaurant last week . . . . Watch those calories, girls!"

The following day, Nancy Lyons came to June in tears. She was terribly upset because she had *not* been drinking coffee. She explained that she was a Mormon and drinking coffee was against her religious beliefs. Her brother had seen the article in the paper and told her parents, who were very angry. They had forbidden her to go to Biffy's any more or to see the friends she had gone with. She felt that she had been terribly wronged.

Your Turn

1. Do you think June's item could be considered libelous? Why?

2. If so, what steps if any, could June take to make up the damage to Nancy?

Libel and the press

June Tanaka did not know that the information she published was damaging. Often, however, the news media are well aware that they have damaging information. Perhaps they have turned up evidence that a public official is corrupt. Or that a football team has fixed a big game. Or that a popular entertainer is a drug addict. Yet they cannot be 100 percent certain that these reports are true.

Suppose they play it safe and publish nothing. Yet it's difficult to be 100 percent certain about *any* critical statement. To avoid libel suits, the news media would have to play it safe all the time.

Does fear of libel threaten the freedom of the press? If so, what can be done about it without threatening the rights of individuals?

The answers differ from state to state. In all states, however, there are special standards for publishers and broadcasters

Charles Oakley kicks dogs and cats

L.S. LOVES H.W.

Richard Weeks is a thief! Greta is a UFO!

Holly Miller is a bird— CHEAP, CHEAP, CHEAP!

Bob, Chuck, Tom, Fred & Buzz are winos!

All Blondes.

when they make statements about public figures. This standard is known as the New York Times Rule. It arose out of a decision made by the U.S. Supreme Court in 1964 in a libel action brought against *The New York Times*.

The New York Times Rule makes a distinction between libel actions brought by private individuals and those brought by politicians, entertainers, sports figures, and so on. Such public figures cannot win a libel action simply by proving that the publisher or broadcaster made a false and damaging statement. They have to prove that the statement was made either deliberately, in the knowledge that it was false, or else with "reckless disregard" for the truth. In effect, this means that public figures have less protection against libel than private ones.

Some courts have decided that the New York Times Rule should also apply to private individuals who are involved in matters of general or public interest.

Read the following case to see how you would decide:

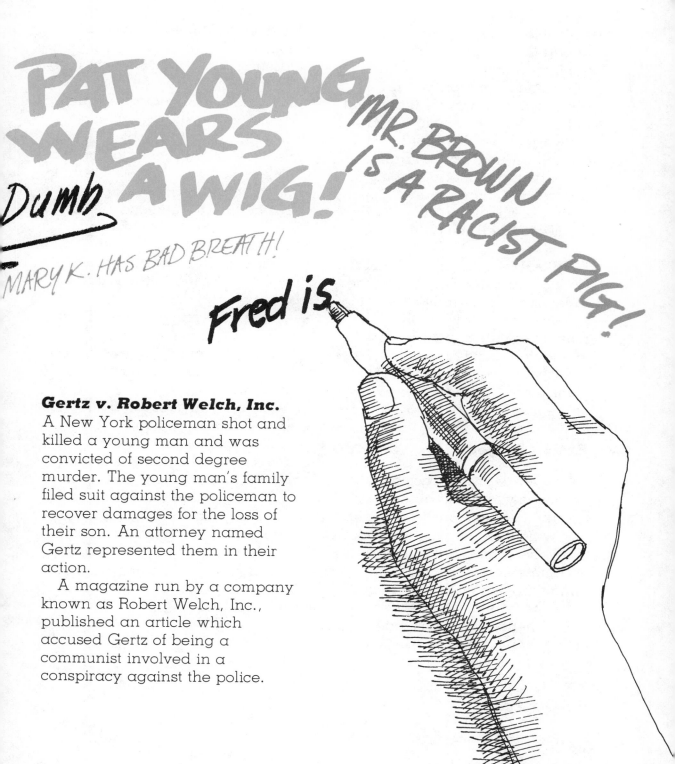

PAT YOUNG WEARS A WIG!

MR. BROWN IS A RACIST PIG!

Dumb

MARY K. HAS BAD BREATH!

Fred is

Gertz v. Robert Welch, Inc.

A New York policeman shot and killed a young man and was convicted of second degree murder. The young man's family filed suit against the policeman to recover damages for the loss of their son. An attorney named Gertz represented them in their action.

A magazine run by a company known as Robert Welch, Inc., published an article which accused Gertz of being a communist involved in a conspiracy against the police.

Gertz filed a libel suit against Robert Welch, Inc. He stated that the information in the article was untrue and damaging to his reputation as a private individual. Robert Welch, Inc. said it had not shown reckless disregard for the truth. It argued that the article was about a matter of public interest and therefore the publisher should be covered by the New York Times Rule.

Your Turn

Do you think the New York Times Rule should generally extend to private individuals involved in matters of public interest? How would you decide the case? Why?

Ask your teacher for the result of this case. It is listed on page 41 of the teaching guide.

Action Project

Look over the list of possible tort situations you made at the beginning of this unit. Cross out any which you now consider not to involve torts. Where possible, add these comments to each remaining situation:

1. The type of tort involved.
2. Whether you think legal action would be justified.

Resource Person. Invite a local media representative to visit your classroom. Your guest might be a local newspaper reporter or a TV or radio newscaster, for example. Ask the guest to talk with you about some of the problems he or she faces in balancing freedom of the press and the people's right to know, with individuals' rights to protect their reputations. Other questions you might ask are:

1. In what situations is the public's right to know more important than an individual's privacy?
2. How carefully do you check your news stories for accuracy?
3. Should public figures have the same protections as private individuals? Why?
4. Have you ever been sued for libel? Can you explain?

After the visit, arrange to have an attorney who handles libel and slander suits visit the classroom to talk with you about such topics as:

1. The procedures followed in preparing a slander or libel suit;
2. How damages are awarded;
3. The range of damages that are usually awarded in slander and libel suits.

"Congratulations!"

Punch — Ben. Roth Agency

The "just married" couple are David and Arlene Smith and the driver of the other car is Burt Brown. The crash could have occurred for various reasons, four of which are listed below. You are the judge when this case comes to court. For each of the four reasons, decide: (a) whether the Smiths or Brown should pay for damages to the other car; (b) whether punitive damages should also be awarded.

1. David was kissing Arlene and had to brake suddenly to avoid a pedestrian.
2. Burt was on his way to a service station to have his brakes fixed.
3. Burt had been in love with Arlene. Angry at being rejected, he deliberately drove into the back of the Smiths' car.
4. Burt had been in love with Arlene. David recognized Burt's car in the mirror and thought he was following them. David stepped on the brakes intending to tell Burt to leave them alone.

The National Pastime, 1889

The Bettman Archive

1. From the evidence of this drawing, have the baseball players so far committed assault, battery, both, or neither?

2. Suppose some friends of the umpire rush to protect him. They knock out three of the players before the umpire has been touched. Do you think the players could win a suit for battery against the umpire's friends? Why or why not?

3. During the game, a player disputes an umpire's decision and shouts, "I'm going to get you for that!" Fifteen minutes later, the player hurls the ball at the umpire's head. The umpire ducks just in time. Do you think he could win a suit for assault against the player?

4. A player disputes an umpire's out call at first base. After a while the umpire yells: "You're a liar and a cheat and you couldn't tell the truth to save your life!" This is picked up by a TV camera and microphone. Do you think the player could win a suit for libel?

Damages, Injuries, and Insults: a Bibliography

The Lawsuit
edited by Donald W. Oliver and
Fred M. Newmann, Xerox, 1968.
Covers various civil law
procedures, focusing on liability,
damages, and settlements.

Youth and the Law
San Diego County Bar Association,
1973.
Covers many aspects of the law,
including torts and family law
(Part 5).

Youth and the Law
by Irving J. Sloan, Oceana, 1974.
Factual coverage of torts, and also
contracts (Part 2) and family law
(Part 5).

171

PART 5
FAMILY LAW

Chapter 11

Marriage and After

You probably think of family life as a private matter having nothing to do with the law. If your brother or sister takes a swing at you or breaks your record player, you don't run for a police officer or an attorney. Most families settle their disputes and make their decisions among themselves.

All the same, the law is very much involved in family life. This isn't surprising. The law deals with relations between people and groups in society, and the family is the basic social unit. Legally, the term "family" applies to any group of people related to one another by blood, marriage, or adoption. And the area of law that covers such groups is known as family law.

Family laws are generally made at the state level. This means that particular laws may differ from one state to the next. However, all states agree quite closely on the areas of family life that should be covered by the law. For example, every state has laws regulating marriage and divorce, and laws dealing with the basic rights and responsibilities of family members. These are areas which are considered important for society as a whole.

At the same time, all states agree on the family's need for and right to privacy. Thus there are many areas of family life that are not governed by law. Such decisions as whether to have children, where to live, and whether to rent or buy a home are left up to each individual family. And except in extreme cases, the state does not usually interfere in everyday family problems.

In this unit, we will approach family law by following one family throughout a lifetime. Chapter Eleven deals with the rights, obligations, and problems of marriage, and also takes a look at divorce. Then children enter the scene. Chapter Twelve explores the legal rights and responsibilities of parents and children. It also covers death in the family and the issue of inheritance.

In short, this unit provides an overview of some of the laws which govern your life as a family member.

Your Turn

We have mentioned some of the areas of family life which are regulated by law and some which are not. What additional areas do you think are governed by law? What additional areas do you think are not? Why?

1.
Deciding to marry

Eileen and Tim had known each other since they were little children. They were very much in love. Everyone knew that one day they would marry.

Tim was a year older than Eileen. When he graduated from high school, he got a job and began to save money. When Eileen graduated, she did the same. Both continued to live with their parents so that they could save most of their earnings.

By the time Tim was 21 and Eileen was 20, they had saved enough money for Tim to open his own auto repair service. The business grew slowly but it was healthy.

They planned to marry on Eileen's 21st birthday. Both sets of parents were looking forward to a big wedding with family members from all over the country.

One evening, as Tim and Eileen talked about their future together, they decided it was silly to wait the ten months until Eileen's birthday. They wanted to marry at once.

Early next morning they took off in Tim's car. They headed for a small town on the coast of Florida, their home state. They planned to get married by a justice of the peace. Then they would honeymoon for a couple of days before heading home.

The two young people were happy and excited as they walked into the courthouse to apply for a license. Their first shock came when they learned that they would have to wait three days. And they would have to pass a blood test, too.

Eileen and Tim hadn't counted on a three-day delay. They had planned to call their parents that afternoon with the good news — after they were already married.

They decided to go ahead and apply for the license. They filled out the forms and handed them to the clerk.

"I'm sorry," the clerk said, "but the young lady is under age. We can't issue you a marriage license without her parents' consent."

Tim and Eileen felt angry. "Look," said Eileen, "I've had a steady job for two years. I'm old enough to know what I'm doing."

"And she voted in the last election," Tim added. "We both did. We're the ones who want to get married, not our parents."

The clerk smiled gently. "I'm really sorry, but that's the law."

They turned and left. "Well, what do we do now?" Eileen asked.

Tim shook his head glumly. "I just don't know."

Your Turn

Tim and Eileen felt angry that they couldn't get married right away, on their own decision. Do you think their feelings were justified? Why?

Marriage and the law

Tim and Eileen found that getting married was not quite as easy as they had thought. As a matter of fact, it is not easy just to describe what marriage is.

Some people consider marriage a love relationship. Some think of it as an arrangement of mutual convenience and companionship. Some see it as a religious commitment. Different people consider it to be many different things. Under the law, however, marriage is considered to be a type of civil contract. Even so, it is unlike any of the contracts we looked at in Part Two.

True, marriage must include offer and acceptance—or mutual consent. And consideration is also involved. In the past, women were expected to bring a gift of money called a *dowry* to a marriage, and men were expected to show that they could support a wife. Today, most couples work out their own financial arrangements. Consideration usually consists of rings given in exchange for promises to do or not do certain things.

How, then, does marriage differ from other contracts? To begin with, it might be described as a three-way contract. It requires not only the consent of the man and woman but also the consent of the state. As Tim and Eileen learned, a couple wishing to marry must meet certain requirements before the state will give its consent.

Of course, the state isn't in the business of matchmaking. It doesn't require that marriage partners be of a particular hair or eye coloring, race, religion, or social standing. It does not require proof of where a couple plans to live, how much they will earn, or what kind of home they plan to maintain.

All states, however, require a marriage license and set a minimum age at which couples may marry. All states also require that a marriage be solemnized by some official ceremony. In addition, many states also require a health certificate and a waiting period between the time the license is applied for and granted.

States may also prohibit

marriages between certain people. For example, in all states it is illegal to marry someone who is already married. It is also illegal to marry a close blood relative, such as a father, mother, sister, or brother. In some states, marriages between first or second cousins are prohibited while in other states they are not. In some states, marriages between step-children, or between step-parents and step-children, are permitted. In others they are not.

Usually, marriages that are legal in the state where they were performed are accepted as legal in all of the states. The same is generally true of marriages legally performed in other countries.

We have seen that a marriage contract is different from other contracts because it requires the consent of the state. But there are other differences as well. The terms of most contracts can be changed at any time by agreement of the parties involved. In fact, most contracts can also be ended that way. The terms of a marriage contract, however, are set by law and cannot be changed. And the contract may not be ended without, again, the consent of the state.

There is another important difference between marriage and other kinds of contracts. In "Minors and Contracts," page 73, we saw that most contracts are not legally binding on minors. Suppose Eileen, as a minor, got her parents' consent and married Tim. Could she later cancel that contract?

The answer is no. If Eileen has her parents' consent and marries Tim, the marriage will be binding.

Your Turn

1. Why do you think the states set marriage requirements?

2. Do you know the minimum ages for marriage with and without parental consent in your state? What do you think is a reasonable age for people to give their own consent to marriage? Write a paragraph explaining your views.

Arranging the wedding

Tim and Eileen were downcast as they started the long drive back to their hometown. But they decided to talk with Eileen's parents that evening and try to obtain their consent.

Eileen's parents listened calmly. They realized that the young people were serious and sincere. At the same time, they felt that Tim and Eileen should give their

friends and relatives a chance to attend their wedding. And since Tim and Eileen came from a strongly religious background, both sets of parents would prefer a religious ceremony.

Eileen's parents asked them to wait for at least a month so that a wedding and reception could be arranged. Tim and Eileen agreed. A month was a lot better than the year they had originally planned.

They reapplied for the marriage license, this time with Eileen's parents' consent and their health certificates. Then they went to speak with their minister about the wedding ceremony.

A wedding ceremony is required for a valid marriage in all states. It may be performed by a justice of the peace. Or it may be a religious ceremony performed by a minister, priest, rabbi, or other religious leader.

In a marriage ceremony, the only legal requirement is that the couple give their names and state that they agree to marry. However, both civil and religious ceremonies usually involve an exchange of vows or promises. Most religious groups follow their own traditional marriage ceremony, but there is no set form for a civil marriage.

Couples may, if they wish, write some or all of their marriage vows themselves. As Tim and Eileen discussed their wedding with the minister, they found some traditional vows they wished to change. For example, they did not feel that Eileen should promise to "obey" Tim. Their minister agreed to reword the ceremony so that they all could accept it.

Resource Person. Invite a local judge who performs marriages to visit the classroom. Suggest that the judge bring copies of marriage license applications and marriage licenses for you to examine and discuss. In advance of the visit, prepare a series of questions you would like the judge to consider. These might include:

1. What are the requirements for marriage in this state?

2. What restrictions are there upon marriage and why?

3. When applying for a license, what kinds of evidence must the applicants present to prove age, parental consent, etc.?

4. What people are authorized to perform marriage ceremonies in this state?

5. How are marriages recorded in this state and why?

6. What procedures do you follow in performing a marriage?

2. Married life

Tim and Eileen's wedding was a happy occasion, with more than sixty of their friends and relatives. The young couple honeymooned in a small beach cottage for a week. Then they returned to their rented apartment to begin making a home together.

Since both had full-time jobs, there were a lot of details to be worked out about their married life. Who would take care of which household chores? Who would take major responsibility for handling the money? How would they budget?

Over the months they worked out most of these details to the satisfaction of both. But they didn't always agree. For example, on her 21st birthday, Eileen gained control of a piece of land that had been left to her by her grandfather. Tim thought she ought to sell it and use the money for the down payment on a house. Eileen wanted to keep the land so that they could build a vacation home there one day. Also, Tim was angry when Eileen contracted for a set of expensive living room furniture without giving him a chance to think it over.

Both found that they had a lot to learn about being a couple rather than two individuals. Still, they had a good relationship and they were able to work out most problems that arose.

Like many young people today, Tim and Eileen looked on their marriage as an equal partnership. They aimed to share both responsibilities and privileges. This is very different from the typical marriage of, say, 150 years ago. In those days, the husband was considered the ruler of the home.

The law took the same view. A woman was entitled to her husband's respect and financial support. But she had little legal say in the marriage relationship.

When a woman married, everything she owned became the property of her husband. Wives were not allowed to make contracts or to go into debt. So in those days, a woman simply could not contract for furniture as Eileen did. Wives could not sue anyone unless their husbands joined them in the suit. In fact, husbands even had the right to discipline their wives when they considered it necessary. For example, if a husband felt that his wife had stepped out of line, he could order her to stay in the house or in her room. And while not many women of those days had jobs outside the home, any income they did make belonged to their husbands.

Today, things have changed. Women have the same rights as men to make contracts and run up debts. Any property they have before marriage remains under their own control. And of course, their earnings do not automatically belong to their husbands.

All the same, the law still has some carryover from the traditional view of married life. Legally, the husband is the head of the family. As the head, he is responsible for the support of his wife. This means that he must provide her with the "necessities" of life, which include food and shelter, clothing, household needs and furnishings, medical and dental care, and even some jewelry. In most states, the husband must provide this support — even if the wife is independently wealthy or has a job with a higher income.

At the same time, the husband has the right to choose where the family will live. And if he decides they will move to another community, city, or state, the wife has to accept his decision.

In many states, the wife has no rights to her husband's earnings beyond the "necessities" of support. However, the husband has no right to her earnings, either. In fact, while he must use at least some of his earnings to support his family, the wife may keep all of her earnings for herself. Any property that the husband or wife gains separately during the marriage remains under his or her own control.

A few states have adopted what is called a *community property* system. This applies to all property, except gifts and inheritances, which the husband or wife acquires during the marriage. No matter who first acquired the property, it belongs under law to both. Usually the property is under the control of the husband. However, each spouse owns an equal share of the property.

181

Your Turn

Many people today feel that laws making the husband "head of household" are dated and unfair to both women and men. Dated because so many wives have jobs and put their earnings into the marriage. Unfair because the laws place too great a burden upon the husband and deny equality to the wife. Do you agree or disagree with the idea of the husband as "head of household"?

Private agreements

Of course, most husbands and wives do not insist on following the letter of the law. They work out their own agreements and their own ways of dealing with problems—much as Tim and Eileen did. And even though husbands may have the legal right to make basic decisions, few of them would ignore strong opposition by their wives.

Usually, husbands and wives are free to make any private agreements within their marriage. The law is involved only if one partner seeks legal enforcement of such an agreement.

And this is where problems may arise. Courts will not allow a contract between a husband and wife which changes the basic terms of the marriage contract. For example, a couple may not legally agree that the husband need *not* provide support.

Here is a case in which a spouse tried to make a private agreement legally binding. If you were a judge, how would you decide it?

Graham v. Graham

Mr. and Mrs. Graham argued a great deal about money. Mrs. Graham was a businesswoman who traveled a great deal and usually her husband accompanied her on her trips. To avoid arguments about money, they agreed that Mrs. Graham would give Mr. Graham $300 a month for as long as the arrangement was desirable to them. When Mrs. Graham stopped the payments, Mr. Graham sued her. He argued that he had given her consideration by resigning from his job so that he could travel with her.

Resource Person. Invite an attorney who specializes in domestic relations to visit your classroom. Before the visit, prepare a list of questions you would like to ask. These might include:

1. Is this a community property

or non-community property state? What are some of the advantages and disadvantages of community property and non-community property laws?

2. What are some examples of agreements between a husband and wife that would be legally enforceable?

3. What are some examples of agreements between husbands and wives that would not be legally enforceable?

3.
Problems in marriage

Tim and Eileen seemed to have a very happy life together. Tim's auto repair business was going well. Eileen had an excellent job doing public relations work. She also handled the accounting for the automotive shop and took care of the advertising.

They had bought a small house and they had heavy mortgage payments. But with both of them working, they still had enough money left over to start saving for a vacation. But then Eileen discovered she was going to have a baby.

They hadn't planned on a baby so soon, and they didn't feel ready to become parents. Eileen enjoyed her career and hoped to begin her own business within the next few years. She did not want to be stuck at home. A baby would mean money problems, too. They didn't see how they could manage if Eileen quit work and then they had the added expense of a child.

They really didn't know what to do. They could see only two ways out of their difficulty, and they didn't like either one.

The first would be for Eileen to have an abortion. This was a choice that would not have been legal a few years ago. Traditionally, abortion laws have been set by the states. In the past, nearly all states outlawed abortion except under special conditions. In some states, abortion was allowed only when it was necessary to save the mother's life. In other states, it was allowed when the pregnancy resulted from rape or incest.

Today, as a result of a Supreme Court decision in 1973, abortion laws in all states are far more liberal. It is now legal for any woman, even a minor, to have an abortion at least in the early stages of pregnancy. However, since many Americans oppose abortion on moral grounds, attempts have been made to change the laws again.

For Eileen and Tim, abortion

was against their religious beliefs. That seemed to leave them only one way out.

This second possibility would be for Eileen to have the baby and then put it up for adoption. In all states, parents may choose to give up a child so that he or she becomes a legal member of another family. They may, if they wish, make their own arrangements with another family, but they must obtain legal approval. Usually, adoptions are arranged through agencies licensed by the state. Either way, the natural parents give up all rights and duties to the child.

Tim and Eileen soon ruled out adoption, too. They knew that once they had the child they would never be able to give it up.

So the nagging question remained: How were they going to manage?

Your Turn

1. Abortion has been a hotly debated issue in recent years. What are some arguments in favor of liberal abortion laws? Against these laws? Which do you agree with?

2. Suppose a married couple is considering abortion or putting a baby up for adoption. Who do you think should make the decision:

the husband (whether or not the wife agrees) or the wife (whether or not the husband agrees)? Or should the decision be made only if they both agree? Why?

Heading for a breakup

The next few months put a great strain on Tim and Eileen. She was sick a great deal and could not continue working past her sixth month of pregnancy. She often slipped into depressions and just couldn't seem to snap out of them.

Tim tried to be helpful and encouraging. But often his efforts just seemed to make things worse. He began finding reasons to stay late at work. This upset Eileen even more.

By the time their daughter Katy was born, Tim and Eileen's marriage was at a very low point. They had spent all of their savings on doctor and hospital bills and they were having a great deal of trouble making their house payments. They seemed to be arguing all the time. Both were miserable. And they needed help.

Couples with problems like Tim and Eileen's can get help from marriage counseling. This kind of service is available through many religious groups and community organizations. There are also marriage counselors in private

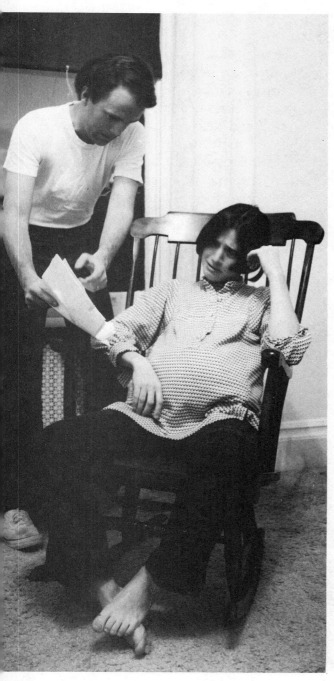

practice. A counselor meets regularly with the couple and encourages them to talk freely about their problems. That way they can find out what their most important problems are and, in many cases, work out their own solutions.

Yet Tim and Eileen still didn't think they needed outside help — until one day they had a jolt. Mike and Samantha, a young couple who lived across the street, announced that they were getting a divorce. And the two of them had always seemed so happy together! Tim and Eileen suddenly realized that their own marriage was at the breaking point.

Your Turn

In all marriages there are areas in which one or both partners must make some adjustments. An unplanned pregnancy created problems in Eileen and Tim's marriage. What are some other areas in which problems might arise for many married couples? Why?

4.
Ending a marriage

Suppose Tim and Eileen decide that their marriage has broken down and they cannot go on

185

living together. What legal steps can they take?

First of all, they are free to make an *informal separation*. For example, Tim might move into a rented room, leaving the house for Eileen and Katy. Legally, they are just as much married as before. Some couples may separate for a short "cooling off" period. Others stay separated for the rest of their lives. Of course, the husband must continue to support the family, and neither can remarry.

Another step is a *legal separation*. This is much the same as an informal separation, except that it is recognized by the state and its terms are agreed upon in a court of law. However, the state will grant a legal separation only for certain reasons. In most states, these reasons are the same as for granting a divorce (which we will look at in a moment).

In special circumstances, couples may be able to obtain an *annulment* of their marriage. A court may grant an annulment when it decides a marriage was never valid under the law. In other words, an annulled marriage is rather like a void contract (see page 77). It is legally considered never to have taken place. Grounds for annulment vary from state to state, but they usually include bigamy (when one partner is already married) and a marriage in which one or both of the partners is under the age of consent.

A *divorce* is granted when a court dissolves or ends a valid marriage. Until 30 or 40 years ago, divorces were quite rare. For one thing most people considered them shameful. And divorce laws were strict. In divorce actions, fault had to be shown. This meant that one of the partners had to prove that the other had done something wrong. And the fault had to be serious. Examples included: adultery, desertion, conviction of a felony, alcoholism, drug addiction, or cruelty.

In the past, even couples with grounds for divorce might choose to avoid the unpleasantness of a divorce action. They might try for an annulment, or make an informal separation, or simply go on living together as best they could.

Today, many couples still prefer these options to divorce. For example, a couple may prefer a separation because of the wishes of their children or because they hope to settle their problems in the end. Or a couple may seek an annulment because their religious beliefs rule out divorce.

However, far more couples today choose divorce as a solution to an unhappy marriage. They no longer consider it shameful. And many states have eased their divorce laws.

In recent years, for example, several states have passed what are called "no-fault" divorce laws. While there still must be cause for divorce, it is no longer necessary in these states to prove that one partner is "in the wrong."

In one no-fault state, for example, there are only two grounds for divorce — incurable insanity and irreconcilable differences. To get a divorce on the grounds of "irreconcilable differences," a couple simply has to state under oath that they cannot solve their problems — whatever these may be.

In some cases, even when there are grounds for a divorce, the court may not grant it automatically. For example, a judge may first order a couple to seek marriage counseling.

Resource Person. Invite a local attorney who specializes in family relations to visit the classroom. In advance of the visit, make up two or three "marriage problems." Ask the attorney to discuss with you the procedures he or she would follow for each case. If any of the problems led to divorce, ask what procedures the attorney would take in preparing the case.

Write a list of additional questions to ask. These might include:

1. What are the grounds for separation, annulment, and divorce in this state?

2. What are some advantages and disadvantages of each?

3. Is this a no-fault divorce state or must fault be shown?

4. What are the residency requirements for divorce and why? How long does it take to get a divorce in this state? Is there a waiting period? Why?

5.
When a marriage ends

The news that Mike and Samantha were splitting up came as a shock to Tim and Eileen. They realized that the same thing could happen to them unless they found help — fast. They spoke with the minister at their church, and he put them in touch with a marriage counseling service. Within days they were sitting in the office of Dr. Harvey Benson, a psychologist and marriage counselor.

While Tim and Eileen discussed marriage problems with Dr. Benson, Mike and Samantha were discussing divorce problems with their lawyers. When a couple decides on a divorce, certain questions have to be settled before the marriage can end. For example: What happens to the property they acquired during their marriage? Who gets custody of the children, if there are any? Should one ex-partner make support payments to the other?

Property settlements

As we have already seen, some states have what is called a community property system. Except for gifts and inheritances, all property acquired during the marriage belongs to both partners. In the event of a divorce, this property must be divided equally between them. For example, if the couple owns a house, each partner is entitled to half of the value—even if the house is in the name of only one. Or, if one partner has started a business during the marriage, the other is entitled to one half of the value of the business.

Suppose for a moment that Tim and Eileen did not solve their problems but got a divorce. If they lived in a community property state, Eileen would be able to keep her piece of land because it was an inheritance. Each would be entitled to one half of the home, however, as well as half of Tim's auto repair shop. This might mean that if the house and the business were of roughly equal value, Eileen would agree to take the house and Tim would agree to keep the business. However, if the business were worth a lot more than the house, Tim might have to sell it or go into debt to pay Eileen her share.

Thus, divisions of community property can be a source of bitterness in divorce cases. Also, it can be a problem to decide exactly what is community property. Often it is difficult to separate property acquired before marriage from property acquired afterward.

In non-community property states, property acquired during marriage can remain separate. Suppose Tim and Eileen lived in a non-community property state and decided to get a divorce. Eileen could, of course, still keep the land she inherited from her grandfather. But if Tim had bought the family home in his own name and also owned the business in his name alone, he might be allowed to claim both as his separate property. And Eileen might not be awarded any share in them. Clearly, non-community property laws can also lead to bitterness.

Of course, many couples try to work out a property settlement that is fair to both partners. But sometimes it involves long and costly negotiations between their lawyers.

Your Turn

We have seen that both community property and separate property can cause problems in the event of a divorce. Which system do you think, on balance, is better? Why?

Support and custody

In the past, most wives depended upon their husbands for support and did not work. Thus, if a couple divorced, the wife was almost always awarded *alimony* — support payments by her ex-husband. Today, however, with so many women willing and eager to work, support payments are not so readily given. And in some instances, it is the husband, rather than the wife, who gains alimony.

In deciding whether to allow support payments and how much to award, a judge will usually take many things into account. These include: the length of the marriage; the age, health, and ability to work of the partner seeking support; whether there are pre-school children to care for; and the ability of the other partner to pay. In states where divorce is based upon fault, the question of who is at fault may be taken into account as well.

Support payments may be awarded for life or for a set period. Usually, however, support payments stop at any time the partner remarries or lives with another as husband and wife.

Suppose the divorcing couple has children, and each partner wants to keep them. Who is given custody?

In the past, young children were almost always given to their mothers unless the mother could be proved "unfit" or did not want custody. That's because courts assumed that mothers have a natural tendency to give better care to children than fathers.

Today, however, that idea is being challenged. In recent years, more and more fathers have won custody of their children in divorce cases.

If the father is given custody, the wife will probably have to pay either a small amount of child support or none at all. However, if the mother gains custody, the husband will almost certainly be ordered to make child support payments.

The amount of child support payments a parent will be asked to make usually depends upon the child's needs and the parent's ability to pay. Child support payments are considered important legal obligations, and failure to pay may lead to contempt of court charges or even to jail. However, child support awards are not final. Either parent can later go back to court to ask for a change in the award.

Unlike support for the ex-partner, child support payments usually continue even if the ex-partner remarries. They end only when the child reaches the age of majority—or, in some cases, when he or she completes college.

The partner who does not gain custody of the children is nearly always granted *visiting rights*. That is, he or she may regularly meet with the children and take them to his or her home.

In some divorce cases, courts may award *joint custody*. This means that the parents take turns looking after the children. For example, one parent may have the children for half the week while the other parent has them for the other half. Or the parents may have the children for alternate weeks, or during different parts of the year.

Your Turn

1. Why do you think child support is considered such an important obligation that failure to pay may lead to jail?

2. Fathers are nearly always expected to pay child support for children not in their custody, while mothers are usually *not* expected to pay. Do you think this is fair? Why?

Action Project

In deciding on custody, the court tries to consider the child's best interests. One state considers the following points:

• How much love and affection there is between the child and each parent.

• To what extent each parent is able and willing to give love, affection, guidance, and education to the child.

• Each parent's ability to provide basic necessities such as food, clothing, and shelter.

• The permanence and stability of each home.

• The moral, mental, and physical fitness of each parent.

• The home, school, and community record of the child.

• The preference of the child, if old enough to make a reasonable choice.

Divide the class into small groups of five to seven students. Have each group discuss the following questions:

1. Do you think some of the guidelines listed are more important than others in deciding who should be given custody? If so, which ones? Why?

2. How much of a voice do you think a child should have in deciding which person will have custody?

3. At what age do you think a child would be old enough to make a reasonable choice?

After the discussion, consider whether there are any guidelines you would add to or take away from the list. Then, as a group, write a list of what *you* think should be the guidelines in deciding who should be awarded custody. Compare your guidelines with those of the other groups in your class. Finally, decide as a class which set of guidelines would be most likely to serve the best interests of the child.

Chapter 12

Parents and Children

By the time their daughter Katy was one year old, Tim and Eileen had a sound and happy marriage once again.

Eileen found that she was able to continue to do the accounting work for Tim's auto repair business at home. She was also able to do some freelance public relations work. This helped ease their money worries and gave her a head start on beginning her own public relations business.

When Katy was two, Tim and Eileen enrolled her in a day care center. Then Eileen sold the property her grandfather had left

her and used the money to launch her new offices.

Tim and Eileen felt that they had a lot to be thankful for. They were happy together. They were both doing well in their work. And they found that they both enjoyed being parents. In fact, they enjoyed parenthood so much that by the time Katy was three, they decided to have another child.

Joseph was born two weeks before Katy's fourth birthday. During his first year, he gave Tim and Eileen much more trouble than his sister had. She had often allowed them a full night's sleep

— while Joseph liked to yell at all hours.

Tim and Eileen often felt exhausted. But they loved Joseph just as much as Katy. And they realized that they were still learning about the responsibilities — and rewards — of being parents.

Your Turn

1. Tim and Eileen felt that parenthood carried many rewards. What do you think some of these rewards might be?

2. What do you think are some of the responsibilities of being parents? Which do you think are legal responsibilities?

1.
Responsibilities of parents

Many of the rewards and responsibilities of parenthood have little or nothing to do with the law. For example, the state does not and could not regulate the amount of affection and love a parent feels for a child or a child for a parent.

Still, parents do have certain responsibilities which are set by law. These apply equally to all of their children, whether natural or adopted.

Providing support . . .

One basic responsibility of parents is to support their children. They must provide the basic necessities of life, including food, clothing, and a place to live. As we saw in Chapter Eleven, this support may be spelled out in terms of money if the parents separate or divorce.

Of course, different parents may have very different incomes. So they are not all held to exactly the same standard of support. But they *are* expected to support their children according to what they can afford.

For example, a wealthy family would be failing in its duty if it raised its children in a tumbledown shack, dressed them in worn-out secondhand clothes, or refused to have their teeth straightened because of the expense. On the other hand, a poor family could not be expected to provide its children with an expensive home, dress them in fancy clothes, or necessarily have their teeth straightened. However, certain minimum standards must be met by all parents.

In most states, the major responsibility for providing financial support rests with the father. This holds true whether the parents are married, separated, divorced, or never married. The

194

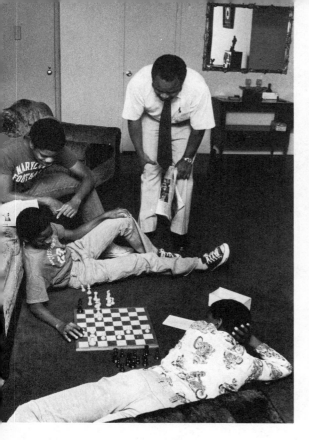

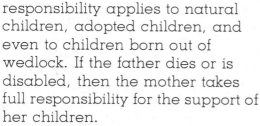

responsibility applies to natural children, adopted children, and even to children born out of wedlock. If the father dies or is disabled, then the mother takes full responsibility for the support of her children.

Of course most parents are more than happy to assume this responsibility. For example, Tim and Eileen would not consider depriving Katy or Joseph of necessities—or of the luxuries they can afford. And countless parents work long hours and make personal sacrifices to support their children.

. . . And care

Another important parental responsibility is to provide care for their children. This is not quite so clear cut as providing support, since it cannot be measured in terms of money. Providing care includes:
• Attending to the physical and emotional needs of childen;
• Providing guidance and a healthful, moral environment;
• Providing proper supervision and control.

Clearly, much of this obligation depends on the values and judgments of individual families.

Still, there are certain guidelines that courts use to decide whether the proper care has been given. And these guidelines tend to reflect the values of our society as a whole.

For example, a healthy moral environment is considered to be based on such values as honesty, fairness, and respect for authority. It is one which encourages children to grow up as useful and law-abiding members of society. The moral environment which Tim and Eileen provide for their children would probably be considered healthy. On the other hand, a home in which the parents are addicted to drugs or alcohol and constantly associate with known criminals would *not* be considered morally healthy.

Supervising and controlling children is an important part of providing care. Here, too, while the details may vary tremendously from one family to the next, certain basic standards must be met. For example, in every state there are compulsory education laws. This means that parents are legally responsible for seeing that their children attend school. If there is a local curfew, parents must see to it that their children are off the streets after that time. And in general, parents cannot allow children to run wild and do anything they want.

To supervise and control their children, parents have the legal right to use whatever *reasonable* means are necessary. In fact, they have a legal obligation to use such means. For example, as we saw in Part Four, parents may be liable for damages if they allow their children to take part in dangerous or destructive activities.

But what are "reasonable means"? These may include "grounding," cutting off an allowance, forbidding the child to associate with certain persons, and even a reasonable amount of physical force.

If parents fail

Just as most parents provide adequate support for their children, so most parents also do their best to provide proper care. But what about those parents who do not or cannot meet their legal obligations? What steps can be taken?

Of course, the state is not in the business of going from door to door checking on families to see whether their children are properly cared for. But there are a number of ways it can find out. If the family receives public aid, a

social worker may be in close touch with the family and its doings. In some instances, relatives, friends, neighbors, or school officials may report that a child is lacking proper care.

If parents are not capable of providing support for their children, they may be eligible for some type of public assistance. For example, they may be able to receive food stamps, rent subsidies, or welfare payments.

If parents are capable of providing support but fail to do so, the court can order them to change their ways. If they still fail, they may face contempt of court charges and possible jail sentences. Of course, sending parents to jail is a last resort, because jailed parents most certainly cannot provide for their children. The court's aim is to see that the children's needs are met.

When parents do not provide the proper care, a child may be declared "neglected." A neglected child may be one who is not given the proper food, clothing, or shelter. It may be a child who is not given adequate medical attention. Or it may be one whose parents have not provided a healthy moral environment.

The state will investigate the situation. If it feels that the child should not remain under the parents' guardianship, it may declare the child a "dependent" child. This places the child under the guardianship of the state.

What exactly does this mean? Where does the child live? Often the child is allowed to remain in the parents' home for a trial period. Or the child may be placed in a relative's home, a foster home, or a state institution.

Sometimes, a child is declared "dependent" for a specific reason and for a set period of time. For example, suppose a school doctor finds that a student has an eye problem requiring surgery. The parents refuse to consent to the surgery because they are afraid of the dangers involved. The doctor could notify local health and welfare officials. If they wished, they could petition (ask) the court to have the child declared "dependent" for the period needed to have the surgery performed. The state could then give consent for the operation.

Still, the state is reluctant to step into this kind of situation. In most instances, a court will not grant a petition to have a child declared "dependent" for purposes of surgery unless the child's life or health is in immediate danger. The state takes the view that in most cases such decisions should be left to the parents.

Your Turn

Parents are held legally responsible for supporting, caring for, and educating their children. Why do you think these responsibilities are regulated by laws? In other words, what is the state's interest in making certain that these obligations are met?

Action Project

The right to an education is considered so important in the U.S. that the states provide free public schooling for all children. And "all" does mean just that. For example, a recent federal law spells out the educational rights of handicapped children. This is the Education for All Handicapped Children Act of 1975. It states that all children with physical or mental handicaps must be provided with free schooling. And the schooling must take their difficulties into account. For example, blind children must be given special texts or recordings.

1. Contact your local education authority to find out what arrangements were made in the past for handicapped children. What new arrangements are being made as a result of the 1975 law?

2. Write a one- or two-page paper explaining why you think the right to a free education is considered so important in the U.S.

Field Activity

Appoint a group of four or five students to arrange a visit to the local Child and Family Services agency. (The agency may go by a different name. You can find out where to call by inquiring at your local health or police department.) The group should interview a case worker at the agency and discuss the procedures that are followed when a case of child neglect is reported.

Another group of four or five students should arrange a visit with a family court judge. They should ask about the procedures followed in the hearing of a neglect case, what the judge looks for in reaching a decision, and so on.

Both groups report back to the whole class. The class should then make up a situation of possible child neglect, and assign students to play the various roles involved. Invite the family court judge to act as the judge in your role-playing. Also, if possible, try to obtain permission to hold the role-playing in the actual courtroom when the family court is not in session.

You be the judge

We have already discussed the right and obligation of parents to control their children. Yet at what point does "reasonable" control become "unreasonable"? Read the following stories. Then decide which of them you think involve reasonable control and which, if any, amount to child abuse.

1. Pam's parents had told her again and again that they didn't want her hanging around Greg, her boyfriend. They didn't like him and they thought that at 14 she was too young to have a boyfriend. One evening she told her parents she was going to the library to study. About 9:30 p.m. her father heard her walking up the steps and opened the door to let her in. Standing just behind her was Greg. Pam's father was angry. Without warning, he

pulled her inside and slapped her so hard that she fell against the wall. Her head was stinging and tears streamed down her face. "Get to your room this second," her father said. "And you, young man, I don't want you to ever come near my daughter again."

2. Jack and his father had never seen eye to eye. But the fight about the family car was the worst yet. His father refused to let him use it and Jack told him he was going to use it anyway.

"You're not quite big enough yet, young man, to tell me what you are and are not going to do," his father said angrily. His father took Jack by the collar of his jacket, threw him into his room and locked the door.

"And you can stay in there, young man, until you're ready to apologize!"

Both Jack and his father were stubborn and both refused to budge. Jack would not apologize and his father would not let him out of his room. By afternoon the next day, Jack was still in his room. He could get to a bathroom for water but he had no food. Jack's mother begged his father to let him out. His father stood firm. "Not until he apologizes," he said.

3. The mother of 12-year-old Johnny worked long hours and

was tired when she got home. One evening as she walked in the door, she thought she smelled marijuana. She peeked into the kitchen to see Johnny carefully drying marijuana in the oven. She felt a sudden rage. She grabbed the closest weapon she could find — a large butcher knife. She held it close to Johnny's throat and screamed that she felt like cutting it. Johnny was terrified. He begged her to put down the knife.

By now she was shaking with sobs and she threw down the knife. But she began beating wildly on his back with her shoe. By the time she was through Johnny was bruised and bleeding. He ran out of the apartment and across the hall to neighbors.

Resource Person. Invite a family relations lawyer to visit the classroom. In advance of the visit, ask the lawyer to read each of the above situations and to discuss which he or she feels are examples of parents acting within their legal authority, which are not, and why. Then ask the lawyer to explain the procedures followed in your state when parents step outside the bounds of their legal authority to control their children.

2. Responsibilities of children

We have talked about the responsibilities of parents. But what about the children? Do they have legal responsibilities, too?

The answer is most definitely yes. Under the law, children have several legal obligations to their parents. In fact, for almost every parental responsibility there is a corresponding child responsibility.

For example, in return for their support and care, parents are entitled to their children's services and to any wages they earn. This means that children have an obligation to do work for their parents and to give their parents any money they earn if their parents ask them for it.

Usually, service to the parents involves normal household chores, such as dishwashing, sweeping, and making beds. And in many cases, parents allow their children to keep their earnings from after school or weekend jobs.

For instance, Katy at the age of 14 and Joseph at the age of 10 were both expected to make their own beds and clean their rooms. In addition, they helped with the dinner dishes each night. Katy also babysat on Friday nights for

the next-door neighbors and was allowed to keep the money for herself.

Still, Tim and Eileen would be within their legal rights if they asked Katy to help out at either of their offices after school for no pay. And they would be entitled to ask her for the money she earned babysitting.

Another important responsibility children have is to obey their parents. For just as parents are responsible for supervising and controlling their children, so are children obligated to do as they are told. Of course, there are limits to this obligation. Children may refuse to obey orders to do something illegal, or something that will endanger a person's safety. But with all normal everyday activities, children are expected to obey.

For example, Tim and Eileen had certain family rules that Katy and Joseph were expected to follow. Joseph was allowed to play in the neighborhood until sunset and then he had to come home. Katy was allowed to visit friends after dinner, if she had finished her homework, helped with the dishes, and let her parents know where she could be reached. But she had to be home by 9 p.m. Since Tim and Eileen were active

church members they also expected Joseph and Katy to attend Sunday School and other church activities.

In general, Katy and Joseph accepted their parents' rules. Of course, like most children, they misbehaved from time to time, or disobeyed a specific order. But they shared their parents' basic standards.

The only really serious disagreement Katy had with her parents during her teen years was over the question of friends. Legally, a parent has the right to tell children with whom they can associate. And on this matter Katy and her parents did not always see eye to eye. One particular dispute involved a young friend of Katy's named Eddie. We will learn more about him in the next few pages.

In special cases, young people can be released from their responsibilities to their parents. If they are married or in military service, or if they make a special agreement with their parents, they can become *emancipated minors*. This usually happens when a young person wishes to control his or her own earnings. At the same time, the parents are released from their responsibilities to the minor.

At school

Another legal responsibility of children is to attend school. As we have seen, it is the parents' responsibility to send their children to school. But it is the children's responsibility to go.

Students must behave properly while they are at school. During school hours, school personnel are considered to "stand in the place of parents." This means that many of the legal responsibilities of parents are transferred to teachers while children are in school. For example, teachers have the right to control and supervise students. This includes setting reasonable rules of student conduct. And in general, teachers and school administrators can use reasonable methods to make certain that these rules are met.

School rules are also set at the state and local level. Therefore, rules may differ from one state to another as well as from one community to another. In most communities, however, teachers have the right to discipline students by keeping them after school, taking away privileges, and even by using reasonable physical punishment. In extreme cases, a school may suspend or expel a student.

When young people go wrong

Most young people break rules from time to time. Normally, parents or teachers take their own action without seeking help from the courts. But sometimes a young person may fail seriously in meeting his or her responsibilities. There may be continual and perhaps criminal misbehavior. And instead of occasionally playing hooky, he or she may continually stay away from school, becoming a truant.

In such a case, the parents or the school may take legal steps. For example, the young person may be brought before a juvenile court. And if the court agrees that the misbehavior has been serious, it may declare the juvenile to be *delinquent*.

If possible, authorities prefer to allow a delinquent to remain in his or her own home and community with conditions as normal as possible. The young person will probably be placed on *probation*. This means that an officer of the court will regularly check to see how he or she is getting along.

In some cases, the delinquent is moved into a foster home. In serious cases, he or she may be moved to a state institution.

Now let's meet Kay's friend Eddie, a boy who had problems both at home and at school.

The problem of Eddie

Eddie, a 13-year-old boy, lived with both of his parents and two younger sisters. He seemed to have every advantage that a young person could want. His parents were well-to-do and had strong church and social ties. And they seemed to care about Eddie's welfare. Still, Eddie was a problem—at home and at school.

He made very few friends and he often got into fights. At school he was known as a troublemaker.

In the seventh grade, he began to cut school two or three days a week. For several months, school officials thought that the absences were due to illness. Eddie would always return to school with a note signed in his mother's name. After repeated absences, the school nurse contacted Eddie's mother to find out more about his health problem.

Eddie's mother was surprised to learn that he had not been going to school. She said that he had not been ill and that she had not signed any absence slips.

When Eddie got home that night, his parents confronted him. At first Eddie denied that he had

"played hooky." Finally he admitted that it was true.

His parents were furious. He was restricted to his room after dinner for a month. Eddie said that he was sorry and would do better in school.

However, Eddie continued to cut school most of each week. And when he did attend, he was still a troublemaker.

Your Turn

1. Eddie continually failed to meet his obligation to obey his parents and to attend school. At this point, what additional steps do you think his parents should take in order to control him?

2. What steps do you think school authorities should be able to take? Why?

3. What do you think should be done if these additional steps fail to control his behavior and correct his truancy from school?

Action Project

The only serious disagreement Katy had with her parents during her teen years was over her friendship with Eddie. Eileen felt that Eddie was a bad influence on Katy and told her that she could not associate with him. Katy felt that it was not fair for her mother to tell her who she could choose for friends.

Have the class divide into small groups to discuss the following questions:

1. Was Eileen within her legal rights as a parent when she told Katy not to associate with Eddie? What arguments could you make to support her position?

2. Would Katy be within her legal rights as a child if she ignored her mother's order about not associating with Eddie? What arguments could you make to support Katy's position?

3. Do you think children should have the right to choose their own friends in most circumstances? In some circumstances? In all circumstances? Why?

Resource Person. Invite a juvenile court judge to visit the classroom to discuss with you the procedures involved in declaring a child delinquent and the steps that are then taken.

Before the visit, make up two to three cases involving juvenile court hearings. These might include, for example, a truant, a child who is continually beyond his parents' control, and a child who has committed a crime.

During the visit, ask the judge to explain to you how each of these cases would be handled and why.

You might also wish to prepare a list of additional questions about juvenile court. These might include:

1. What are the most common types of cases that come before you?

2. How are most of these cases handled?

3. How many "delinquent" children are there at present in this community?

3.
Planning for the future

By the time Katy was 18 and Joseph was 14, Tim and Eileen decided it was time for them to make some plans for the future. When they consulted an attorney, he was surprised to learn that neither Tim nor Eileen had made out a will. Of course, they were both still young—not quite 40—and didn't expect anything to happen to them. But the lawyer pointed out that if something *did* happen, they would need a will to make certain that their property was settled the way they wanted.

He explained that if either of them died without a will, their property would be distributed according to the laws of the state. And while these laws are

...signed to be fair, they might not agree with Tim and Eileen's own wishes.

Tim and Eileen decided they would write wills. They spent the next few days thinking about what they would want to have done in the event of their deaths. For example, if they both died, who should look after Katy and Joseph? What arrangements should they make for the children's further education? Who should take care of the businesses?

After discussing these questions, they returned to the lawyer and told him what they wanted. He went over each question carefully and arranged to have their wills drawn up.

He also explained that they could change the terms of their wills or write new ones any time they wished. This made Tim and Eileen feel better about the whole matter. They knew that in a few years their situation could change. They might have grandchildren they would want to include in their wills.

The next five years were happy ones for Tim and Eileen. And luckily, nothing happened to either of them. Katy went off to college and Joseph entered high school.

Four years later, Katy came home from school with the announcement that she planned to be married in the fall. Her parents were delighted. It seemed like only yesterday that they themselves had decided to marry.

Your Turn

1. Like many people, Tim and Eileen waited until their children were almost grown before they made out a will. Why do you think many people wait so long to make out wills?

2. Why do you think the state handles the distribution of property of people who die without a will?

3. Adopted children have the same rights of inheritance as natural children. However, in many states, children born out of wedlock have the right to inherit only from their mothers but not their fathers. Do you think this is fair? Why?

Resource Person. Invite a lawyer who specializes in wills to visit the classroom. Ask the lawyer to talk with you about:
• The importance of wills;
• What makes a valid will in your state;
• How property is distributed in your state when someone dies without a will.

Family Law: a Bibliography

Youth, Law and Life

Wyoming Area School District, 1971.

One section deals with family law.

Under 21: A Young People's Guide to Legal Rights

by Michael Dorman, Dell, 1971.

Covers many areas, including parent-child rights and responsibilities.

Up Against the Law

by Jean Strouse, New American Library, 1970.

Questions and answers in many areas of the law, including contracts (Part 2), marriage and family.

CONCLUSION

What YOU Can Do

This book is not meant to teach you how to be a lawyer. Its purpose is to give you an understanding of your rights and responsibilities as an American citizen.

There are many rights and responsibilities. Some are simple, others extremely complex. Some go back hundreds of years in the form of common law or case law. Others have been — and are still being — written by our federal, state, and local legislatures.

If people feel that they are being denied their legal rights, they can take action under the law. They can bring a suit to regain their rights and, in many cases, be compensated for their loss.

Taking action

As we saw in Unit One, the simplest way to take legal action is to bring a suit in Small Claims Court. But with many cases this is not possible. The amount at stake is too high, or the legal issues involved are too complex. Then the person bringing suit has to hire an attorney or a team of attorneys. And he or she must be ready to spend a lot of time and risk a lot of money on the case.

If a person is considering a legal action, where does he or she begin? How can you tell if it's worth your while to bring a suit? The first step is to talk with a lawyer. If you do not know a lawyer, you can call or write to the nearest bar association. Tell them the area in which you need help (for example, housing law or negligence), and they will give you the name of a local lawyer who is familiar with that area. You can ask that lawyer for a consultation. (Most lawyers charge only a moderate fee for this service.) The lawyer can then tell you if you have a case.

If you decide to bring a suit, it will most likely go to a state court. Each state has its own judicial system, but there are usually three levels of courts. Your suit will probably be heard in a lower court, or "court of original jurisdiction." If you are dissatisfied with the result, you can go to a state court of appeal. And if you are still dissatisfied, you can take your case to the third and highest level, which in many states is called the state supreme court. The U.S. Supreme Court can also be appealed to from the state system. However, it hears only a limited number of cases, usually those which raise issues of constitutional importance.

While most suits are brought by single individuals or groups, it is also possible to bring a case on behalf of many individuals. Such suits are known as *class actions*. For example, suppose a company owned many apartment buildings and failed to provide proper maintenance. If just one tenant sued, the company might think it worthwhile to pay him or her damages and do nothing to improve conditions. But if that tenant organized a class action, the company might have to pay damages to all tenants — perhaps thousands of them. Thus, in some cases a class action can be much more effective than an individual action in righting wrongs.

Student participation

As we have seen, laws often change to meet the changing needs of society. It is possible for each one of us to take part in those changes.

One area in which students have played an effective part is consumer law. Dawn Ann Kurth is

214

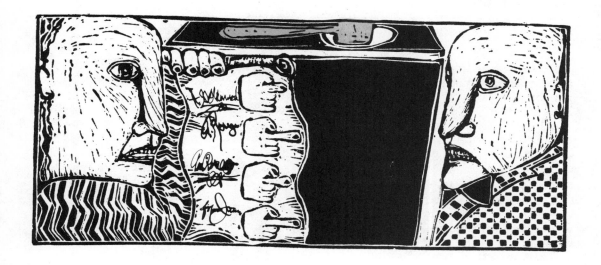

one of 36 students in Melbourne, Florida, who organized a special school research project in this area. She studied the effects on children of TV commercials in children's programs.

Her interest began when her little sister asked their mother to buy a cereal that offered a free record. The cereal was duly bought, but the record didn't work the way it had in the commercial. "I realized then," says Dawn, "that here was a problem I could do something about—or, if I couldn't change things, at least I could make others aware of deceptive advertising practices to children."

She kept a count of the number of commercials on Saturday morning TV shows and made a note of any claims that seemed deceptive to her. She also sent questionnaires to students in other schools, asking for reasons why children bought certain items.

As a result of her thorough study, Dawn was asked to testify before the U.S. Senate Subcommittee on Consumers. In other words, her findings were being listened to by the people who make our nation's laws.

Your Turn

What areas of the law are of most concern to your class? What action do you think you could take to make your views known to lawmakers and the public? What effect do you think this action might have?

Glossary

Acceptance. One of the steps in making a contract. It takes place when one person accepts an offer made by another. For example, Sue offers to sell Mary her watch for $25. Mary says, "Fine, I'll take it." Mary's statement is an acceptance. (See also *Contract* and *Offer*.)

Action. Filing suit in a court of law to correct a wrong. Same as *Lawsuit*.

Alimony. An allowance given by one spouse to the other (usually by husband to wife) after they divorce. (See also *Divorce*.)

Annulment. A court decision that a marriage was never valid.

Bait and switch. A deceptive advertising practice. Customers are "baited" into a store by an ad promising a product or service at a low price. Sales clerks then "switch" them to a more expensive product or service.

Battery. Harmful or offensive contact by one person with another person without consent. It is one kind of *Intentional tort*.

Bigamy. The crime of marrying a person while still married to another.

Binder. In a real estate transaction, a written agreement in which the buyer and seller state their intention to complete the sale.

Breach. The failure of any party to a contract to meet all of its conditions. For example, Joe borrows $20 from Jim and promises to pay back $5 a week. There is a breach of contract if Joe misses a week's payment. (See also *Contract*.)

Case law. Laws made by courts. For example, after a case is decided by the U.S. Supreme Court, lower courts will then use this decision in ruling on similar cases. The Supreme Court's decision has thus become a kind of law.

Caveat emptor. Latin for "Let the buyer beware." This was the rule in buying and selling in the past. In other words, it was up to the consumer to protect his or her own interests. The rule has faded somewhat with the rise of consumer law. (See also *Consumer law*.)

Cease and desist order. An order to stop a harmful or illegal practice. For example, the Federal Trade Commission may order a business to stop airing a deceptive TV commercial. (See also *Federal Trade Commission*.)

Child support. In a divorce action, the children are usually put in the care of one of the spouses. Child support is the payment made by the other spouse to help provide this care.

Civil law. Laws which deal with the private rights of individuals, groups, and businesses. Civil laws describe what people can do if they feel they have been wronged by another person, a business, or the government. They do *not* deal with crimes. (See also *Criminal law*.)

Class action. A lawsuit brought by one or more individuals on behalf of an entire group of people. For example, suppose a customer believes that a public utility is providing poor service to a whole community. That customer may bring a class action against the utility on behalf of all its customers. A class action can be more effective than a suit filed for just one person. Suppose the court awarded damages against the utility. Those damages would have to be paid to all consumers, not just to the one who filed the class action.

Collateral. Something of value used as security for carrying out a contract. (See also *Security*.)

216

Comparative negligence. A rule used in many states to decide negligence cases where both parties are at fault. For example, two cars collide because both drivers are careless. If one driver was less negligent than the other, he or she might be awarded some damages. (See also *Damages* and *Negligent tort*.)

Consideration. A basic part of a legal contract. It is something of value given in exchange for something else. For example, if Sue offers her watch to Mary for $25 and Mary accepts, the consideration is the $25. (See also *Contract*.)

Consumer Credit Protection Act. A 1969 federal act requiring businesses that give credit to tell buyers *exactly* what their credit costs. They must give full details of interest and other charges.

Consumer law. Laws which affect the buying and selling of goods and services.

Contempt of court. Obstructing justice — for example, by refusing to obey a court order. An individual found in contempt of court may be fined or sent to jail.

Contract. A legal agreement between two or more parties. It consists of an *offer*, *acceptance*, and *consideration*. In many cases, a spoken contract is just as legal as a written one. (See also *Statute of Frauds*, *Offer*, *Acceptance*, and *Consideration*.)

Corrective advertising. Advertising that corrects a misleading statement in earlier ads. The Federal Trade Commission may order such corrections from businesses that use deceptive advertising. For a period of time, the businesses must state in their ads that the previous advertising was deceptive.

Common law. The legal customs and court decisions formed in England and later in the U.S. over several centuries. Common law provides the basis for the system of law used in the U.S.

Community property. The laws of several states consider married couples to have an equal share in all property (except gifts and inheritances) acquired during their marriage. If a couple divorces, the property must be divided equally between the two.

Co-sign. To guarantee that a contract made by someone else will be carried out. For example, a person who co-signs a loan promises to make the payments if the borrower cannot do so.

Counter-offer. A step that may take place in making a contract. When one person makes an offer, the other person may suggest a change. For example, when Sue offers Mary her watch for $25, Mary may say: "I'll give you $20." This is a counter-offer. (See also *Contract*.)

Credit rating. Estimate of a person's ability to repay credit. It is usually based on the person's income and past payment record. There are special organizations which keep records on people who have obtained credit. (See also *Fair Credit Reporting Act*.)

Criminal law. Laws which describe crimes and the penalties for committing them. Court actions under criminal law are brought by the state. This is different from civil law, in which actions are brought by individuals or groups.

Custody. Responsibility for the care of children. In a divorce case, the court decides which parent will have custody— that is, with which parent the children will live. (See also *Child support*.)

Damages. Compensation awarded by the court as the result of a civil action. For example, a person injured in a car crash may sue the driver for damages.

Deed. A signed document which changes property from one owner to another.

Default. Failure to do what is required by law. It usually applies to the failure of a defendant to appear in court. This results in a default judgment, which means that the plaintiff wins the case automatically. (See also *Defendant* and *Plaintiff*.)

Defendant. The person against whom an action is brought.

217

Delinquent. A young person who breaks the law or is beyond the control of his or her parents.

Dependent child. A minor who is removed from his or her parents and placed in the custody of the state. For example, a minor who is treated brutally by his or her parents may be made a dependent child. (See also *Minor*.)

Divorce. A court decision ending a marriage.

Equal Credit Opportunity Act. A federal act passed in 1974 and expanded in 1977. The act makes it illegal for lenders to refuse credit for such reasons as: sex, marital status, race, religion, and age — if old enough to apply for credit. It also requires lenders to give reasons for denying credit.

Eviction. A legal procedure for taking over land or housing. For example, a tenant may be evicted if he or she fails to pay rent.

Fair Credit Reporting Act. A 1971 federal act entitling consumers to find out what is in their credit record. Among other things, it also allows them to have incorrect information removed from the record. (See also *Credit rating*.)

Fair Housing Law. A federal act passed in 1968 and expanded in 1974. Under this law, landlords renting four or more units may not refuse tenants on the basis of race, religion, national origin, or sex.

Fair Packaging and Labeling Act. A federal act passed in 1968. It covers any products that are shipped across state lines. Such products must be labeled and packaged honestly and informatively.

Federal Trade Commission (FTC). A federal regulatory agency created in 1914 to support fair business practices. Today the FTC also plays an important role in consumer protection.

Felony. A serious crime which is punishable by more than one year in jail.

Finance charges. An extra charge to consumers for buying on credit.

Foreclosure. A legal way of taking back sold property. A seller can foreclose when the buyer fails to keep up payments.

Gross negligence. Extreme carelessness. In certain civil actions, gross negligence may lead to higher damages. (See also *Damages* and *Negligent tort*.)

Installment loan. A loan which is repaid in installments, often in equal monthly amounts.

Intentional tort. A deliberate action which harms another person's body, property, or rights.

Interest. The money charged for a loan.

Invalid. Not recognized by the law. For example, a contract made for an illegal purpose is invalid. It cannot be enforced in a court of law.

Joint custody. A court decision that more than one person take care of minors. For example, in a divorce action, both parents may be awarded custody of their children. (See also *Custody*.)

Juvenile court. A state or county court that deals with cases involving young people. The age limit for juveniles varies from state to state.

Lawsuit. See *Action*.

Lease. A legal agreement between the owner of property and the tenant who wishes to rent it. The lease states how long the tenant will rent the property and how much he or she will pay.

Legal separation. A separation of husband and wife arranged in a court of law. (See also *Separation*.)

Lessee. A person to whom property is rented.

Lessor. A person who rents property to another.

Liability. Legal responsibility for an illegal or harmful act.

Libel. Writing, printing, or broadcasting false information that is damaging to a person. (See also *Slander*.)

Majority. The age at which a person is legally considered an adult. It varies from state to state, but is usually between 18 and 21.

Market research. Studies of consumers made to help businesses improve and/or sell their products.

Minor. A person under the age of majority.

Misdemeanor. A crime that is less serious than a felony. It is punishable by a fine and/or imprisonment in county jails. (See also *Felony*.)

Mortgage. A method of borrowing money to buy a house. The borrower signs over the house to the lender as security for the loan. If the loan payments are not kept up, the lender can take possession of the house.

Negligent tort. A wrong or injury suffered by one person as a result of another person's carelessness. (See also *Intentional tort*.)

New York Times Rule. A rule affecting libel actions brought by public figures (such as politicians and entertainers). To win a libel action, a private person only has to show that the defendant made a false and damaging statement. But a public figure also has to show that the statement was made with "actual malice." The rule arose out of a Supreme Court Decision in *New York Times Co. v. Sullivan*. (See also *Libel*.)

No-fault divorce. In most states, a married couple can obtain a divorce only if one of them shows "fault" in the other — for example, desertion. In some states, however, a couple may get a divorce without the "fault" being put on either of them.

Nuisance. Using one's home or other property in an unreasonable way which damages another person's rights. For example, someone who keeps neighbors awake at night by playing the drums is committing a nuisance.

Offer. The first step in making a contract. It is a promise by one person to do something in exchange for something from another person. (See also *Contract*.)

Out-of-court-settlement. An agreement by both sides in a lawsuit that settles their dispute before it goes to court.

Party. A person or group of people involved in a legal agreement or proceeding.

Petition. A request for a court order. For example, a relative or social worker may petition the court to have a child declared dependent. (See also *Dependent child*.)

Plaintiff. The person who brings an action against another. (See also *Defendant*.)

Probation. A period of time in which a person's behavior is checked. For example, in a child neglect case, the parents may be allowed to keep their child for a certain time. During that time a social worker checks to see whether the behavior of the parents has improved.

Punitive damages. Extra damages intended to punish the defendant. Plaintiffs often ask for punitive damages in lawsuits involving intentional torts. (See also *Intentional tort*.)

Quiet enjoyment. The right to occupy property without interference. For example, a tenant is entitled to quiet enjoyment of a rented home.

Reasonable person. The standard used by courts in negligence cases. The defendant is found negligent if he or she failed to use the care expected of an average "reasonable person." (See also *Negligent tort*.)

Rental agreement. An arrangement to rent property on a month-to-month basis. Either the landlord or the tenant can end the agreement on a month's notice. (See also *Lease*.)

Repossess. To take back property from a person who fails to meet the terms of possessing it. For example, if someone buys a car but fails to make the payments agreed upon, the seller may repossess the car.

Revolving credit. A type of credit often used by department store and bank credit cards. Each month the consumer can pay part of the amount owed for purchases, plus interest.

Security. Something of value put up as a guarantee that the terms of a contract will be met. For example, a savings account may be used as security for a bank loan.

Security deposit. Money deposited by the tenant with the landlord for the length of a lease or rental agreement. It can be used to pay for any breakage or abnormal wear and tear caused by the tenant.

Separation. An informal agreement between husband and wife to live apart. (See also *Legal separation*.)

Sheriff. A county official who enforces the laws.

Slander. The spreading of false and damaging information about a person by word of mouth. (See also *Libel*.)

Small claims court. A special court for cases involving small amounts of money. It enables people to settle these cases quickly and inexpensively.

State courts. Courts in the judicial system of each state. They usually include: courts of original jurisdiction, state courts of appeal, and a state supreme court.

Statute of Frauds. A law adopted in most states requiring that certain types of contracts be in writing. For example, a contract must be in writing if it cannot be completed in less than one year.

Strict liability. Legal responsibility which does not depend on negligence or intent. For example, a trucker who is carrying explosives is strictly liable for any injury they may cause. It does not make any difference if the trucker was using all possible care. (See also *Negligent tort* and *Intentional tort*.)

Subpoena. An order for a witness to appear in court or to produce evidence for use in court.

Sue. To file a lawsuit. (See also *Lawsuit*.)

Title. Legal ownership of property. A person who owns his or her own home has a document which shows title to the property.

Tort. A wrong or injury committed by one person against the body, property, or rights of another. (For examples, see *Battery*, *Libel*, and *Trespass*.)

Trespass. Deliberately going onto another person's land without right or permission.

True annual percentage rate. The total interest rate charged per year for a loan or credit purchase.

Truth-In-Lending Law. A popular name for the Consumer Credit Protection Act. (See also *Consumer Credit Protection Act*.)

Uniform Commercial Code. A law standardizing the various state laws that cover business activities. At this time, the Uniform Commercial Code has been adopted in some form in nearly every state.

Valid. Recognized by law. For example, a valid contract is one that can be enforced in court.

Violation. The breaking of a rule or law.

Visiting rights. The right of a divorced parent to see children in the custody of the other parent. (See also *Custody*.)

Void. Non-existent under the law. For example, a void contract legally never existed.

Voidable. An agreement which may be declared void. For example, a contract between a minor and an adult can usually be canceled by the minor. It is a voidable contract.

Will. A written document in which a person says what should happen to his or her property after he or she dies.

Index

PHOTO CREDITS: Page 2, 12, Fred Burell • 15, 22, Richard Hutchings • 24, 25, 26, 27, Carlos Castro • 28, 29, 32, 34, Richard Hutchings • 38, Photo Researchers/Ray Ellis • 40, 41, Richard Hutchings • 58, Fred Burell • 61, 63, 74, 75, Richard Hutchings • 78 (top), Culver Pictures; (bottom), Richard Hutchings • 80, 82, Richard Hutchings • 88, Fred Burell • 91, 92, 109, Richard Hutchings • 11, Photo Researchers/Bob Combs • 112 (top), Photo Researchers/Bom Combs; (bottom), Photo Researchers/Katrina Thomas • 114, Photo Researchers/Bruce Roberts • 124, Fred Burell • 126, 129, 139, 140, 159, 164, Richard Hutchings • 172, Fred Burell • 175, Richard Hutchings • 178, Nancy Timbers • 185, 186, Richard Hutchings • 192 (top), Photo Researchers/Rohn Engh; (bottom), Monkmeyer/David Stricker • 195 (left), Monkmeyer/Mimi Forsyth; (right), Monkmeyer/Sybil Shakman • 200, 203, Richard Hutchings • 205, Magnum/Ron Benvenisti • 207, 209, Richard Hutchings.
COVER: Fred Burell • Insert photo: Dan Nelken